T0311787

Military Spending and Global Security

Global military expenditure reached an estimated $1,822 billion in 2018 and this book questions what that spending responds to and indeed what that entails in terms of global security.

The book draws from prior knowledge and research on military expenditure but introduces an all-encompassing, in-depth and original analysis of military spending as a key and often overlooked factor of global instability, delving into the present and future consequences of its perpetual growth, as well as confronting the reasoning behind it. The authors argue that increasing military expenditure is not the best response to the emergencies militarization itself has helped create. They assert that militarization is paradoxically both a cause of and a response to the grave challenges our society is facing. The book explains why people are not well served by nation-states when they continuously seek to out-compete one another in the size and destructive powers of their militaries. It discusses the scope of military spending around the world, while explaining how militarism is linked with conflict and security threats, and how military spending further prevents us from adequately dealing with global environmental problems like climate change.

A must-read for scholars, researchers and students from a wide range of disciplines. It will also find an audience among professionals from the third sector and activists working on issues related to peace, security and militarism, as well as social and climate justice.

Jordi Calvo Rufanges is vice-president of the International Peace Bureau, coordinator of the Global Campaign on Military Spending, professor of armed conflicts, defence economy and international relations and coordinator and researcher of the Centre Delàs of Peace Studies, Barcelona, Spain.

Routledge Studies in Defence and Peace Economics

*Edited by Keith Hartley, University of York, UK and Jurgen Brauer,
Augusta State University, USA.*

For a full list of titles in this series, please visit www.routledge.com/
series/SE0637

Military Spending and Global Security

Humanitarian and Environmental Perspectives

Edited by
Jordi Calvo Rufanges

Routledge
Taylor & Francis Group

LONDON AND NEW YORK

First published 2021
by Routledge
2 Park Square, Milton Park, Abingdon, Oxon OX14 4RN

and by Routledge
52 Vanderbilt Avenue, New York, NY 10017

Routledge is an imprint of the Taylor & Francis Group, an informa business

© 2021 selection and editorial matter, Jordi Calvo Rufanges;
individual chapters, the contributors

The right of Jordi Calvo Rufanges to be identified as the author
of the editorial material, and of the authors for their individual
chapters, has been asserted in accordance with sections 77 and 78 of
the Copyright, Designs and Patents Act 1988.

All rights reserved. No part of this book may be reprinted or
reproduced or utilised in any form or by any electronic, mechanical,
or other means, now known or hereafter invented, including
photocopying and recording, or in any information storage or
retrieval system, without permission in writing from the publishers.

Trademark notice: Product or corporate names may be trademarks
or registered trademarks, and are used only for identification and
explanation without intent to infringe.

British Library Cataloguing-in-Publication Data
A catalogue record for this book is available from the British Library

Library of Congress Cataloging-in-Publication Data
Names: Calvo Rufanges, Jordi, editor.
Title: Military spending and global security : humanitarian and
environmental perspectives / edited by Jordi Calvo Rufanges.
Description: Abingdon, Oxon ; New York, NY : Routledge, 2021. |
Series: Routledge studies in defence and peace economics | Includes
bibliographical references and index.
Identifiers: LCCN 2020025636 (print) | LCCN 2020025637 (ebook)
Subjects: LCSH: Armed Forces—Appropriations and expenditures. |
Military readiness—Economic aspects. | Military policy—
Economic aspects. | Militarism. | Human security.
Classification: LCC UA17 .M57 2021 (print) | LCC UA17 (ebook) |
DDC 355.6/226—dc23
LC record available at https://lccn.loc.gov/2020025636
LC ebook record available at https://lccn.loc.gov/2020025637

ISBN: 978-0-367-49339-4 (hbk)
ISBN: 978-1-003-04582-3 (ebk)

Typeset in Bembo
by codeMantra

This publication is a part of the International Peace Bureau and Centre Delàs for Peace Studies project in the framework of the Global Campaign of Military Spending which counts with the support of Ajuntament de Barcelona.

With the support of

Contents

Figures

Tables

Notes on contributors

Mark Akkerman is a researcher at Stop Wapenhandel (Dutch campaign against arms trade) and author of several reports on border militarisation and the military industry (in cooperation with the Transnational Institute). His research has also been focussed on arms exports to the Middle East, the private military and security sector, greenwashing arms trade and the militarisation of development cooperation.

Colin Archer was the Secretary-General of the International Peace Bureau in Geneva from 1990 to 2017. Among several major programmes over this period, he inaugurated the International Peace Bureau (IPB)'s work on Disarmament for Sustainable Development, out of which was born the Global Campaign on Military Spending. He is the author of *Warfare or Welfare?* and *Whose Priorities?*

Pere Brunet is a Retired Professor from the Polytechnic University of Catalonia. He is a researcher at the Centre Delàs for Peace Studies. He has a special interest in the interrelation between ethics, science and technology with a focus on Peace and Global Justice. His recent publications include the Drones Report 'Novel Weapons against Ethics and People'. He has been involved in the IPB Global Campaign on Military Spending (GCOMS) Campaign.

Jordi Calvo Rufanges is an economist, researcher on peace, disarmament and defence economy. He's Coordinator of the Centre Delàs for Peace Studies and armed conflicts, defence economy and peace and security lecturer in several universities. He is Vice-President of the International Peace Bureau (IPB) and Coordinator of the Global Campaign on Military Spending (GCOMS).

Tarja Cronberg is a Distinguished Associate Fellow at Stockholm International Peace Research Institute (SIPRI) (nuclear disarmament, security architecture of the Persian Gulf). She is the Chair of the Finnish Peace Union, Vice-President of the IPB and a Board member of the European Leadership Network. Her books include *Nuclear Multilateralism and*

Iran: Inside EU-Negotiations, Nuclear-Free Security and *Transforming Russia: From Military to a Civil Economy.*

Aude-E. Fleurant is an Associate Researcher at the Belgium-based Groupe de recherche et d'information sur la paix et la sécurité (GRIP, Research Group on Peace and Security). She previously worked at (SIPRI) as the Director of the Arms and Military Expenditure Programme.

Joseph Gerson is President of the Campaign for Peace, Disarmament and Common Security and Vice-President of the International Peace Bureau. His books include *With Hiroshima Eyes: Atomic War, Nuclear Extortion and Moral Imagination* and *Empire and the Bomb: How the U.S. Uses Nuclear Weapons to Dominate the World.*

Chloé Meulewaeter is a researcher of the Centre Delàs for Peace Studies, and a PhD student in Peace Culture at the University of Granada, Spain. Her investigation focusses mainly on the relationship between military spending, the arms trade and armed conflicts.

Alejandro Pozo Marín is a peace, armed conflicts and disarmament re-searcher. He has PhD in peace and conflicts with a thesis on new wars and their global factors. He has worked as an armed conflict analyst and as humanitarian projects coordinator. Has carried out on the ground researches in several countries in war situations. He is a peace and armed conflicts professor in several courses and masters.

Yannick Quéau is Director of the Groupe de Recherche et d'Information sur la Paix et la Sécurité (GRIP, Brussels). He was previously Head of research in the same organisation. His work covers international security, transatlantic relations, the industrial, strategic and economic aspects of the arms trade, whether conventional or nuclear, and arms control.

Laëtitia Sédou runs the EU military research Programme of the European Network Against Arms Trade (ENAAT). She has been following and ana-lysing EU policies for more than 20 years on behalf of human rights and peace organisations.

Bram Vranken is a researcher and campaigner with the Belgian peace or-ganisation Vredesactie. He works on topics related to the arms trade, EU defence initiatives and defence lobbying. He is the author of the report 'Securing Profits – how the arms lobby is hijacking Europe's defence policy'.

Dave Webb is chair of the UK Campaign for Nuclear Disarmament, Vice-President of the International Peace Bureau and Convenor of the Global Network Against Weapons and Nuclear Power in Space. He is also an emeritus Professor at Leeds Beckett University where he was Professor of Engineering from 2003 to 2010 and then Professor of Conflict Studies from 2010 until he took retirement in 2012.

Tom Woodhouse is Emeritus Professor in the Department of Peace Studies and International Development at the University of Bradford, UK, and Visiting Professor in the Faculty of Communications and International Relations at the University Ramon Llull Barcelona. He is member of the International Advisory Council of the Institute for Economics and Peace and has published widely, including *Contemporary Conflict Resolution*, co-authored with Oliver Ramsbotham and Hugh Miall.

Acknowledgements

I would like to thank all people who have made possible this publication. First of all authors deserve my gratitude, their contributions have been done with wisdom and generosity, with a common objective, using knowledge and reflection for a more peaceful world. I also want to thank all Centre Delàs for Peace Studies and IPB team for their support and contribution, primarily to Quique Sánchez for being always so helpful and efficient when it has been required, the same as Jorge Guardiola for opening the possibility of this edition. I also have to mention with special emphasis my gratitude to Colin Archer, one of the authors and also a solid support in contents and edition of this book. I finally want to dedicate this work to Sara for her unconditional support, and specially to Lluc and Kai, the main reason to persevere working for peace.

Foreword

Tom Woodhouse

This is a remarkable and a very welcome book, one which is not only of its time but also very much for our times. We now live in a period of turbulent change, of rising populism and nationalism, a time of eroding and weakening multilateralism, of the militarisation of borders and the construction of walls between nations and communities. The world faces four existential threats: the increased dangers of nuclear proliferation and nuclear war (threat 1); climate change and the challenge it presents not only to social order but also to life itself (threat 2); an escalating arms race and a global military industrial complex which now accounts for world military expenditure at its highest level since the Cold War, reaching 1.82 trillion USD in 2018, or 2.1% of global GDP (threat 3). As the Institute for Economics and Peace has shown, military expenditure, while it is the largest component of the global cost of violence, is only a part of the global cost of containing violence which stood at US$14 trillion, or 12% of world GDP. A 1% reduction of this expenditure is the equivalent of the total Official Development Assistance in 2017. This level of military spending widens the gap between rich and poor, distorts development globally, fuels armed conflict and provides one strong explanation for a further dynamic of destabilisation, the forced migration of 67.75 million people in 2017, fleeing persecution, violence and poverty (threat 4).

So this book is indeed timely, an opportunity to refocus, to take stock and to widen our understanding of the systemic challenges we face. The year 2020 is the 75th anniversary of the bombing of Hiroshima and Nagasaki. It is also the 75th anniversary of the formation of the UN, which for all its imperfections provided a rules-based order internationally, including respect for territorial integrity, in which international law prohibited wars of aggression, and where a network of multilateral treaties tried at least to contain and manage strategic competition in arms. If there is a systemic breakdown in world order, this book provides a wake-up call for fresh thinking. By looking at the problem systemically, as this book encourages us to do, we have the opportunity to think and act beyond the narrow competing nationalisms and big power rivalries to vision of what has been called 'Peace writ Large'.

From this perspective, another anniversary needs to be noted. In this case, 2020 marks 225 years since Immanuel Kant published *Perpetual Peace*, his classic thesis against nationalism and realpolitik (which drove aggression, militarisation and arms races), in favour of enlightened cosmopolitanism. Kant made the important distinction between what he called a pactum pacis – (a peace pact) – and a foedus pacificum (a pacific federation), where the former aims to stop specific wars, and the latter to end warfare. While Kant's ideas seem remote from us in time, they remain salient for our challenge to respond to the global insecurities posed by the re-energised militarism which is re-emerging, and others have built on his thinking. We also have the tools, networks, methodologies and epistemologies, thanks to a generation of peace research and action, which were not available to Kant. It is also 60 years since Lewis Fry Richardson published the first scientific surveys of Militarism and Arms Races, in *Arms and Insecurity*, and in *Statistics of Deadly Quarrels*, and 50 years since Johan Galtung provided his definitions of peace and conflict structures in his terms negative and positive peace, and direct, structural and cultural violence.

We now have a knowledge base and rich and diverse datasets which can be used to measure, model and predict patterns of conflict formation and ways of measuring peace and peacefulness. It is 50 years since the Department of Peace and Conflict Research at Uppsala University in Sweden developed their first Conflict Data Programme, 15 years since the Institute for Economics and Peace produced the first Global Peace Index (to measure peacefulness in societies) and five years since they published the first Positive Peace Index, outlining an Eight-Pillar model to define the nature and content of peaceful relations (defined as the 'attitudes, institutions and structures that create and maintain peaceful societies').

With tools and resources such as these we can turn with renewed confidence to address the challenges presented by resurgent militarism, and we should be grateful to the editors and contributors to this commendable volume for defining so clearly the nature of the challenge. The analysis is presented in eight chapters, covering trends and drivers; links between Military Expenditure (ME) and conflicts; ME and military operations abroad; the Moral Budget and campaigns to contain ME; militarisation and the EU; the cost of nuclear weapons; ME and climate change; and the evolution of peace movement thinking on ME. Taking this body of knowledge collectively as an explanation for the contemporary manifestation of the drivers and consequences of a security paradigm re-establishing itself as the power to impose negative peace (direct violence), we are in a much better position now to counter this and transform our understanding of security as a goal related to human security and positive peace.

Introduction

Jordi Calvo Rufanges

We are facing a new, wide and deep process of militarization worldwide. Military budgets are increasing every year, arms exports show a constant growth, military industry keeps expanding and more countries are capable of producing weapons. Investing in arms is very profitable; public grants and loans for research and development of new weapons are being increased; the NATO military alliance pushes member states to dedicate 2% of their GDP to military budgets; migrations and borders, among others, are also more militarized than ever.

As an extension of the Cold War idea of deterrence and security doctrines based on an increase in military capabilities as a way to get more security, militarization in the 21st century is creating a new arms race. Growing military arsenals and the strength of military capabilities in more countries are promoting mistrust and suspicion among the entire international community, moving International Relations back to old paradigms that were already outdated, based on anarchist (Realist) relations among countries, conceptualized on competition and balance of power. All this is occurring despite article 26 of the Charter of the United Nations, which recognizes the need to "promote the establishment and maintenance of international peace and security with the least diversion for armaments of the world's human and economic resources".

This backward trend occurs in part due to the influence of economics related to arms races and militarism, which can be studied from a defence economics approach. We can define this concept and a related one, the military-industrial complex, a term used to refer to all actors involved in such business, adding a framework that explains the dynamics of these actors and the consequences of the evolution of an economic sector with military interests, and of a military with interests. It is the so-called military-economic cycle, which is explained from a theoretical point of view and from its main data that shows the volume and relevance of military spending, arms transfers, arms industry and financing of weapons production worldwide.

Defence economics and the military-industrial complex

Defence economics is defined as a set of measures that cause the transformation of the economic structure of a country aimed at addressing security and defence needs, focussing mainly on offensive actions like a war, or the assumption of deterrence through the arms race in order to avoid future armed conflicts.[1] Taking into consideration that economics deals with the allocation of scarce resources to different destinations and purposes, scarcity can therefore be the starting point of defence economics and the reason why the concept of opportunity cost is crucial to understand the importance of the decisions made.[2]

Defence economics maintains a relationship with the discipline of international relations as well as economics in areas such as government budget, public goods, trade and industry. In fact it exists in the intersection between economics and international relations and pays attention to key strategies such as the allocation of scarce resources in a given economy.[3] Defence economics also focusses on the study of the efficiency of resources allocated to military needs,[4] which can be analysed by examining the military structure to achieve the objectives of security and defence. Moreover, defence economics incorporates industrial policy related to military matters and pays special attention to the management of the business sector related to the production of weapons or performing services in armed forces.[5] Thus, military-industrial complex will be the term used to refer to this sector.

"Military-industrial complex" came into use in Eisenhower's farewell speech as US president in 1961, when he referred to power of the lobbyist with the most influence in the White House. The military-industrial complex is made up of people, business and political organizations, including senior military officers of the departments or ministries of defence, who influence decisions on military policy, including armaments purchases. The military-industrial complex is based on interests that put pressure on policies to raise military budgets in order to ensure the present and future of a specific sector: defence economics.

The major shareholders and executives of companies that supply governments' defence departments compose the military-industrial complex.[6] It includes arms businessmen, middlemen, but also military officials and politicians. In addition, military companies have a complete network of think tanks physically based close to the main centres of political decision-making, with hundreds of military lobbyists in Brussels and Washington, which help politicians and civil servants on security matters through publications, reports, conferences, congresses and recommendations about defence and security.

The military–economic cycle, definition and volume

The military-economic cycle is composed of a network that encompasses all aspects surrounding the military structure of a country, which include the security and defence policy of a state that determines the national defence strategy, and the military model. This model will determine what kind of infrastructure, facilities, equipment and military dimension are necessary.[7]

The military lobbies participate in defence economics through the military-economic cycle, which is the term that describes the economic conglomerates around defence economics.[8] It is a cycle that describes the route that weapons production takes, from the decision to take resources from the military public budget to cover the alleged need for weapons to their final use.

Defence policies are set by the definitions of national objectives, and by the military and diplomatic means that a state has at its disposal to fulfil a self-assigned role on the international stage.[9] The beginning of the cycle starts in the discourses and arguments that legitimize the need for arms and armies and, thus, justify high levels of militarization and armaments.[10]

The need to possess armed forces is determined by the geopolitical strategy of each country, influenced by its geostrategic situation and the international military and political organizations to which it belongs, and also depends on the culture of defence, militarized education, military and arms history and tradition, and tolerance for weapons and military forces in a society.

Therefore, the first step of the so-called military-economic cycle is the military spending. It has reached the highest level since the end of the Cold War: 1.8 trillion USD is Stockholm International Peace Research Institute (SIPRI)'s estimation for 2018, representing 2.2% of global GDP and 230 USD per person per year. As usual, a few countries account for most of the military spending, accounting for 60% by the first five (the USA, China, Saudi Arabia, Russia and India). By regions it is North America (40%) leading this ranking, followed by East Asia (18.6%) and Western Europe (14.1%). Europe and Asia together account for 45% of global military spending. Military budgets are mainly used to cover the cost of the armed forces' human resources and their weapons and equipment – there are 16.5 million military personnel and 11.9 million paramilitary forces in the world, but also to keep and foster the military economic sector.

Another main part of the military-economic cycle is composed of arms producers and their exports, which reach 30,000 million USD of major weapons every year, according to SIPRI's data. How does the arms export sector work? Most of the military companies are private and try to get contracts from any government that is willing to buy, but arms trade is not a free market, it is highly regulated by international and national norms and treaties. Military industries cannot sell weapons if their government doesn't allow them to do so. The main regulations for arms trade are focussed on criteria that forbid arms exports licences to countries in conflict, with instability or where human rights are violated. In spite of that, every year arms are sold to countries engaged in conflicts and war and violate human rights, such as Saudi Arabia and the UAE, members of the military coalition in the Yemen War, Turkey, Egypt, Iraq, Afghanistan and many others that are far from peace or an example of respecting human rights. The main importers of arms in 2018 are Saudi Arabia, India, Egypt, Australia, Algeria, China, the UAE, Iraq, South Korea, Vietnam, Pakistan and Indonesia.

There are thousands of arms companies in the entire world, but as in many other sectors, few of them dominate global military markets. The first 100 arms industries identified by SIPRI are producing arms worth about

400,000 million USD every year. Regarding their origin, the main arms companies come from the main military expenditure and arms exporting countries: 57% are from the USA, 9.5% from Russia, 22% from Western Europe, but also from Japan, Israel, India and South Korea. As we can see, the major arms producers are NATO countries and other military allies. But there are new countries that are investing in a future national military industry, through imports that combine the acquisition of costly weapons systems with the transfer of technology and production of part of them in their own national territory. That is the case of Australia and what Saudi Arabia is attempting to do.

Financing of arms is also an important issue in the military-economic cycle. Military companies are financed by banks, insurance companies and investors, through many of their products: loans, revolving credits, bonds issuance, shareholding, etc. We know from the *International Armed Banks Database* that financing of some of the main arms companies in the world has reached 526,000 million USD in the period 2013–2018, with the participation of more than 500 banks, from 30 countries.

National security and militarization

National security has been defined by Walt (1991)[11] as the study of threats, use and control of military force, from a state-centric and militarist viewpoint, revitalized since the Global War on Terror. The traditional military and political understanding of security is that in the military sector, the reference point is the state itself, whereas in the political sector, existential threats are identified as those that affect the constituting principles of the state and its sovereignty.[12] The cultural concept of national security is developed, as the "grouping of knowledge, norms, values, goals, attitudes and socially shared practices directed at protecting and guaranteeing national interests".[13]

A recent example of how military responses may not the best response to fight against security threats is the so-called "Global War on Terror" due to its failure getting more security through military interventions. Nobody doubts the need for an answer after the 9/11 attacks in the USA and hundreds of terrorist attacks of a similar nature in Europe, Asia, Africa and Middle East. The main military power worldwide, the USA, drove the so-called Global War on Terror, which gave rise to the military occupation of Afghanistan and Iraq by the US Army and its allies, and direct and indirect military interventions in Libya, Syria, Mali or Yemen, among others.

Among all threats identified by most national security and defence doctrines all over the world, terrorism is arguably the main threat to security. Terrorist threats are much higher nowadays than when the Global War on Terror started, in 2001.

To better understand the most relevant risk factors and threats to security, we can study those identified by the defence strategies of the EU, NATO,

Spain and the USA. To do so, we follow the analysis of the latest doctrines of security and defence from Calvo Rufanges (2018: 8–9).[14]

> All of them identify the following threats to security: terrorism and violent extremism, proliferation of weapons of mass destruction, cyber-security, energy security, organized crime, maritime security – and in the case of the US this extends to air and outer space – ,climate change, irregular migratory flows – and in the case of the EU, the management of external borders, and economic crises – which NATO specifies as financial. The US adds economic slow downs as security threats. Finally, elements which all of them seem to have in common, in the analysis of risks or threats, are armed conflict and the so-called weak or failed states.
>
> It is, however, important to mention some other security concerns identified in these four doctrines that are relevant. The EU also mentions the threats and risks to security posed by pandemics and epidemics, poverty and inequality, human rights violations, and the dual threat of changes in the equilibrium of economic powers and globalization and the interdependence it brings. As for NATO, they also include demographic changes that could be worsened by global problems like poverty, hunger, pandemic disease, as well as the previously mentioned dual threat of globalism and interdependence.
>
> As well, the US has expanded their identification of threats and security risks to include what it calls global outbreaks of infectious disease, with the possibility of a catastrophic attack on American soil or basic infrastructure; attacks on its citizens on foreign soil or against its allies, to which has been added extreme poverty, genocide, or what have been termed mass atrocities, as well as the impact of globalization and interdependence or changes in economic power. The Spanish government has also identified several threats to security: the vulnerability of critical infrastructures and essential services, protection against emergencies and catastrophes, espionage and counterintelligence, security in the aeronautical and railroad sectors and globalization.
>
> In addition to the aforementioned threats and risks, it is worth adding countries or regions identified in the doctrines studied as potential security threats. All of them consider Russia to be a country of special concern, and in practically all of them with more or less emphasis you find the Middle East, Africa and specifically the north of Africa, Maghreb and the Sahel, and the Democratic People's Republic of Korea, Iran, and the Arctic. In greater detail, the EU mentions the western Balkans and Turkey, while the US pays particular attention to China. Spain also gives a special mention to the British colony of Gibraltar.

The previous analysis of threats and risks to security places us in a scenario in which military responses seem a marginal resource of doubtful utility in terms of confronting all threats mentioned above, because they are already tackled through diplomacy, police, environmental measures, humanitarian action and social services, among others. It can be argued that what makes up the basis for national security policy are existing tools, which far from being only military or police, have more to do with diplomacy and foreign policy, and include international cooperation for development, the economy, health, education, justice, social services, civil protection, intelligence, etc.[15] Moreover, in words of Mutimer (2007)[16] security is not a given, objective and unquestionable dimension, but rather it is susceptible to any number of interpretations, and as a result, analysis on the topic is not neutral from a moral or political viewpoint. In the same direction, Booth (1991)[17] affirm that when individuals are the defining standard of security states become unreliable providers of security.

Military security is not the best response to the challenges faced by our modern, global, interdependent and diverse society. Weapons are inherently ambiguous in a political and strategic sense, since their real strength is based on the generation of mistrust.[18] Theoretical foundations and practical approaches point towards the possibility and necessity of building a theory and practice of security based on different parameters that are an alternative to and even opposed to the hegemonic security state that encourages the military-economic cycle. Arms businessmen are the most interested in the promotion of securitization, as the best scenario to keep up their economic activity and profit.

An epistemological approach is necessary, as security analysis is not neutral.[19] The military-industrial complex is not neutral. We need to acknowledge its power to influence security policies, through political work to increase military spending in public budgets; through making control of arms exports more difficult; through their relations with banks that are supporting arms companies with diverse means of financing; and through ensuring they are beneficiaries of grants and public support to military research.

The efficiency of military responses to security threats is under scrutiny. Military companies are able to get from government's public contracts, grants for military research and support from foreign affairs services from the Ministry of Defence, and even from Heads of States, thanks to the influence of the so-called military-industrial complex. Military budgets militarize relations between countries. More militarization means bigger armed forces, easier to mobilize, to be sent anywhere in the world. High rates of military spending make more likely the use of military instead of diplomacy. As a result, cooperation, multilateralism and preventive diplomacy are at risk of being totally ineffective. Military budgets are the only relevant source of incomes for military industry. Thus, arms businessmen need to keep the military security approach in governments to assure their activity and future profits.

Securitization is not done only in relation to migration policies, but also to some of the main challenges for humanity, like climate change. If everything is placed under a securitization perspective, military responses will be more likely. Securitization considers all social, human or environmental aspects as military threats and militarized solutions, which is definitely the best marketing strategy for the arms industry. Moreover, defence economics has to pay attention to how military spending responds to security threats to a given country or city, identifying whether there are parts of the military budget that have no direct relation to the real needs of security.

This book's objective is to analyse some of the main aspects of defence economics as drivers for militarization and arms build-up that are by themselves factors that increase the likelihood of the use of armed force. In order to introduce a critical approach to securitization and the influence of the military-industrial complex, eight chapters compose the analysis of this compilation. Defining military spending as a starting point of the abovementioned military/arms economic cycle, it is important to consider the approach to the "Trends in worldwide military spending", where Fleurant and Quéau analyse the weight and evolution of this indicator worldwide. The second chapter analyses the interactions that occur in the functioning of the cycle. In this case, Meulewaeter proves, through a quantitative methodology, how military spending may have a casual relation with arms exports and armed conflicts. As a continuation of the previous chapter, Pozo looks more deeply at the impact of military spending on the likelihood of developing military operations abroad from a perspective of the antiterrorist doctrine adopted after 9/11. The fourth and fifth chapters are showing the volume of militarization of security in the regions with the highest military spending: the USA and the European Union. The authors Sedou, Vranken and Akkerman are explaining in an extensive chapter the new developments of military spending and security policies within the new budgetary framework of the European Union. Gerson offers a critical analysis of the American military spending as a tool of foreign policy of a country that depends on its military power to enforce its foreign policies. The seventh chapter, written by Brunet and Meulewaeter, presents a much-needed approach to the relevance of military spending and some of its consequences such as climate change, that in part stem from a hegemonic model of growth worldwide in which militarization has a key role. Finally, Archer explains the responses coming from civil society through the historical evolution of the global campaign on military spending, GCOMS, which was created and promoted by the author of the chapter, giving also attention to related pacifist challenges to militarization emerging from social movements.

Notes

1 Hartley, K. (2007), "Defense economics: Achievements and challenges", *Economics of Peace and Security Journal*, vol 2, núm 1, pp. 45–50.
2 Dabelko & McCormick (1977), "Opportunity costs of defense: Some cross-national evidence", *Journal of Peace Research*, Peace Research Institute Oslo, vol 14, num 2, pp. 145–154, June.
3 Sandley, T. y K. Hartley (1995), *The economics of defense*, Cambridge University Press, Cambridge.

4 Viñas, A. (1984), "Economia de la defensa y defensa económica: una propuesta reconceptualizadora," *Revista de Estudios Poíticos (Nueva Època)*, vol 37, January–February.
5 Fonfría, Antonio i Pérez-Forniés, C. (2013) (coord.), *Lecciones de economía e industria*, Madrid, Civitas Thomson Reuters.
6 The role of trade unions is also very important, because by defending the preservation of their jobs, they put pressure on governments to increase military spending and allocate it to the arms contracts in those industries where they are working.
7 Calvo Rufanges, Jordi and Alejandro Pozo (2015), *Diccionario de la guerra, la paz y el desarme*, Barcelona, Icaria.
8 Calvo Rufanges, Jordi and Alejandro Pozo (coord.) (2009), *Atlas del militarismo en España*, Barcelona, Icaria; Oliveres, Arcadi i Ortega, Pere (2000), *El ciclo armamentista español*, Barcelona, Icaria.
9 David, Charles-Philippe (2008), *La guerra y la paz. Enfoque contemporáneo sobre la seguridad y la estrategia*, Icaria, Barcelona.
10 The Olin Foundation, with funds coming largely from the US military industry, gave grants totalling US$370 million to neoconservative ideology projects for half a century, in George, Susan (2007), *El pensamiento secuestrado*, Barcelona, Icaria.
11 Walt, M. (1991), "The renaissance if security studies," *International Studies Quarterly*, vol 35, num 2, June 1991, pp. 211–239,,in Perez de Armiño, Karlos and Mendia Azkue, Irantzu (2013), *Seguridad humana. Aportes críticos al debate teórico y político*, Madrid. Visiones críticas.
12 Buzan, B., Waever, O. and Wilde J. (1998), *Security. A new framework of analysis*, Lynne Rienner Publishers, London, p. 23.
13 De la Corte, L. and Blanco, J.M. (2014), *Seguridad nacional, amenazas y respuestas*, LID, Madrid, p. 36.
14 Calvo Rufanges, Jordi (Coord) (2018), *Políticas de seguridad para la paz. Otra seguridad es posible y necesaria*, Barcelona, Icaria.
15 De la Corte, L. and Blanco, J.M. (2014), *Seguridad nacional, amenazas y respuestas*, LID, Madrid, p. 36.
16 Mutimer, D. (2007), "Critical security studies: a schismatic history" in Alan Collins, ed., *Contemporary security studies* (Oxford: OUP, 2007), pp. 53–74, in Pérez de Armiño, Karlos. and Mendia Azkue, Irantzu (2013), *Seguridad humana. Aportes críticos al debate teórico y político*,Tecnos, Madrid.
17 Booth, K. (1991), "Security and emancipation," Review of International Studies, vol 17, num 4 pp. 313–326, in Buzan, Barry and Hansen, Lene (2015), *The evolution of international security studies*, Cambridge University Press, Cambridge.
18 Booth, Ken and Wheeler, Nicholas J. (2008), *The security dilemma. Fear, cooperation and trust in world politics*, Palgrave Macmillan, New York.
19 Perez de Armiño, Karlos and Mendia Azkue, Irantzu (2013), *Seguridad humana. Aportes críticos al debate teórico y político*, Madrid. Visiones críticas.

1 Trends in global military expenditure

Drivers of increases and causes of concerns

Aude-E. Fleurant and Yannick Quéau[1]

1.1 Introduction

In 2018, global military expenditure was firmly on a growth path from 2014, the lowest level of the 2010 decade. Since 2014, funding allocated to the military increased by 5.6% by 2018[2] and is–for the time being–expected to continue to rise in the coming years. The expansion of resources given to the military since 2014 in Western countries such as the United States (US) and Europe's largest spenders (France, Germany, the United Kingdom (UK)) are attributed to a shift from concerns over the economy to narratives of a volatile and dangerous international security environment (Congressional Research Service, 2019). Threat perceptions of China and Russia displayed by Western States and partner countries in other regions such as Australia and Japan are partially spurred by a so-called 'new era of great-power competition' (Wong, 2019), a narrative that is reminiscent of both world wars and the Cold War. As a result, the pessimistic portrayal of the current security landscape contributes to the legitimation of increased military spending, which, in turn, may feed into regional and global tensions.

This chapter presents and discusses global, regional and national trends in military expenditure and their main contemporary drivers. The national level section addresses mostly the largest spenders in the world and explores other cases in other regions and sub-regions. Finally, it discusses issues related to transparency in military expenditure and concludes with a critical comment of militarism and military spending.

1.2 Structure, drivers and key actors

A significant feature of global military expenditure is the remarkable stability of the hierarchy of the largest spenders, as was seen even during the 2008–2009 financial crisis. Indeed, despite economic or security crisis impacts leading to decreases in their military expenditure, the largest spenders tend to remain at the top, minus or plus one or two ranks depending on the years. Over a ten-year period, a group of only eight states have occupied the Top five to seven positions. In 2009 and in 2013, the same group of countries were listed in the top seven spenders, namely the US—which has occupied the first position permanently—followed by China, France, the UK, Russia, Japan, Germany. As a comparison, the first seven largest spenders in 1989 were the US, the Union of Soviet Socialist Republics (USSR), France, Germany, the UK, Japan and Italy. The stability at the highest ranks is remarkable; so are the scope and influence of these countries on the global trend. The top five in 2018 accounts for 60% of total spending, with a combined figure of $1.1 trillion. For the same year, the top ten largest spenders account for 74% of global military expenditure. Together, these countries 'make' the global trend in military expenditure. Interestingly, the hierarchy of largest spenders in each region reproduces this structure. For all regions, a handful of countries dominate total regional military expenditure, as shown in this chapter's section on regional and sub-regional expenditure.

The stability in the rankings highlights another core feature of military expenditure, namely the very slow pace of changes at the head of the list while smaller spenders tend to move ranks more often as changes in smaller military figures tend to create higher variations between countries' expenditure. This is why looking at regional and sub-regional military expenditure and highlighting dynamics and situations of some of the countries in those regions provides more nuanced insights into the dynamics of military expenditure.

As a general rule, phases of increases can be attributed mainly to a handful of core drivers, primarily wars/security concerns, arms modernization programmes and military reforms such as professionalization of the armed forces, and to any combination of those. In States from the Western Hemisphere, arms modernization cycles tend to occur about the same time, and usually span decades. When projects or reforms are implemented, or involvement in conflicts comes to an end, military funding tends to decrease. For example, the end of the Cold War hastened the decline of the 1980 Reagan Build-up.[3]

The state of the global and/or national economy is also a decisive factor in military budgeting, as major economic events such as recessions tend to change military expenditure trajectories. The financial crisis of 2008–2009 led to decreased military spending in countries such as the US and several Western European countries, notably the UK. London relies partly on financial services for its revenue, as it represents a 6.9% share of the total country output. Following the decline due to the financial crisis and loss of government revenue, military expenditure declined by 17% from 2009 to 2018.

However, it did not have a visible impact on African and South American military expenditure, which continued to grow until 2014, a year when the price of commodities crashed which led to decreases in the military expenditure of countries for which primary resources are a significant part of the national revenue. One such case is Angola, which showed a military spending drop of 67.8% in 2018 compared to 2014 due in large part to the fall in oil prices.

1.3 Global military expenditure

In 2018, Stockholm International Peace Research Institute (SIPRI) estimated that total military expenditure reached $1822 billion, the highest figure reported since 1989. The five largest spending countries account for 60% of total military expenditure; the ten largest spenders for 74% of the total, leaving 26%, or 528 billion to the remaining 145 countries for which data was available in 2018.[4] The 2018 increase compared to 2017 is driven by growth in military expenditure in the Americas (+4.4%) and Asia and Oceania (+3.3%), while Europe's military spending rose more moderately (+1.4%) and Africa's decreased (−8.4%). For four consecutive years, SIPRI has not provided a regional military expenditure estimate for the Middle East, due to a severe lack of transparency in some of the states' figures, such as Saudi Arabia's, and due to the fact that some of the largest regional spenders, such as the Qatar and the United Arab Emirates (UAE), have not provided military expenditure figures. Global military spending growth is attributed to increases by the largest spenders in the context of increased political-strategic tensions and participation in active wars, as well as to the concurrent start of major weapons modernization programmes.

At the time of writing this chapter, the global economy was showing signs of potential contraction, notably from two of the largest economic and military powers, Germany and the US. Moreover, according to reports (He, 2019), China's economic growth rate was slowing down in 2019 due to the commercial war between the US and China. Even though these countries have planned to increase their respective military expenditure, if a recession materializes, it could slow down or thwart military spending growth.

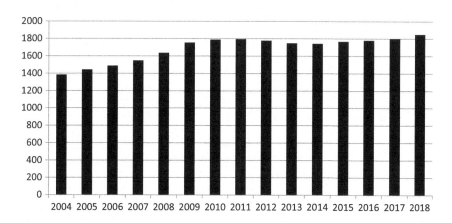

Figure 1.1 Global military expenditure 2004–2018.

Note: Figures are in US$ billions, at constant 2018 prices and exchange rate.

Source: own elaboration.

1.4 Regional and sub-regional dynamics

Regions and sub-regions display specific profiles in terms of military expenditure and their drivers. Looking at spending evolution over a ten-year time-frame reveals broad trends and what supports them, as well as their weight in global military spending. All regions are presented in alphabetical order.

Even though *Africa* includes the highest number of countries[5] of all regions,[6] it is the smallest regional spender with a share of 2.2% of total military expenditure. Africa's military spending increased by 9.2% over a ten-year period, despite a significant decline of 16.4% from 2014 to 2018 due to the 2014 drop in commodity prices. The decline in revenue hit mostly sub-Saharan countries and consequently, military expenditure was reduced by 26% from the peak of 2014 to 2018. In 2018, the military spending of the 47 sub-Saharan African states for which SIPRI has figures accounted for almost half the region's military expenditure with 45.3% of the region's total. The four remaining countries of North Africa show a slightly higher share of the continent's spending with a share of 54.6% share of the region with 22.2 billion in military expenditure.[7] Countries in North Africa are the largest spenders in Africa, notably Algeria, with a spending of $9.6 billion, followed by Morocco with $3.7 billion. No figure has been available for Libya since 2014. Other large spenders in sub-Saharan Africa are Kenya with $1.1 billion, Nigeria $2.0 billion and South Africa $3.6 billion.

Overall, the continent continues to struggle with several conflicts and enduring tensions. In North Africa, Algeria and Morocco are still at odds on Western Sahara, a situation that has been ongoing for almost 50 years. Libya is in a civil war over, among other things, the control of oil. In sub-Saharan Africa, estimates of the current number of conflicts range from 10 to 15, depending on the definition of armed conflict. The Sahel countries are

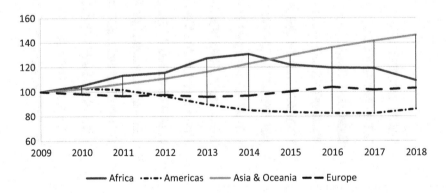

Figure 1.2 Regional military expenditure – relative changes (percentages) base 100, 2009–2018.
Source: own elaboration.

fighting insurrectional forces and the Great Lakes Region countries fight over land and exploitation of natural resources. As a general rule wars, whether national or transnational, civil or between countries, tend to increase funding for the military. Nevertheless, this analytical tool does not necessarily apply systematically for sub-Saharan African countries due to the specificities of each context or system of conflicts (terrorism in Sahel, tensions around the Great Lakes, maritime security on the Eastern coast). The participation of major foreign countries in these wars is a critical factor of differentiation since in many cases these countries assume the main costs of military operations.[8] France, for instance, has been involved in the Sahel-Sahara alongside G-5 Sahel armed forces.

Considering the modest levels of military expenditure in sub-Saharan Africa, an interesting and clearer way to look at the sub-region countries' spending is to look at the share of a country's military expenditure on its gross domestic product (GDP), also called the military burden. This indicates how much of the country's wealth is assigned to the military. For example, the Republic of Congo's military expenditure of $292.3 in 2018 was equivalent to 2.5% of its GDP, a somewhat high figure compared to its closest neighbours' military burden such as the Democratic Republic of Congo (0.7%) and Gabon (1.5%).

The Americas' military expenditure[9] is heavily influenced by the US military expenditure trajectory, as it is by far the largest spender in the world. With expenditure of $648.8 billion in 2018, the US accounts for 88.3% of the region spending, for 96.8% of the North American sub-region, and for 35.6% of global military outlays. Central ($8.6 billion) and South America's ($55.6 billion) sub-regional military expenditure is dwarfed by the North. Central **America** includes 13 countries, some of which, such as Costa Rica and Panama, do not have a military force and therefore have no military budget. Mexico is, by far, the largest spender in Central America, dominating the sub-region with a share of 77% of the total. South America's spending, with 11 states, is $55.6 billion, making 7.6% of the region as a whole. The largest spender in South America is Brazil, with $27.8 billion in 2018. Part of the importance of the country's spending is military pay, which mobilizes a significant share of Brasília's military budget, a remainder from the dictatorship. Moreover, the country endeavours to produce large weapon systems indigenously, with the assistance of major military–industrial European countries such as France. The second largest spender in South America is Colombia, which is struggling with another domestic armed conflict and with enduring criminal violence linked to the drug trade.

Considering the size of US spending, with a total of $648.8 billion in 2018, the country not only the country dominates the region, but also its spending is large enough to have an impact on the global trend. This seems to have been the case from 2010 to 2014; global military expenditure decreased by 2.0%, while US expenditure declined by 19.5% for the same years. Although US spending is very high, it was 19% lower in 2018 than at the peak of

2010. Mexico has been affected by the commodity prices crisis, with a drop of 18.2% from the high of 2015 to the low of 2017, interrupting substantial military spending growth of 100.7% from 2004 to 2016. In South America, the heavyweight spender is, by far, Brazil, with a share of 50% of total South American expenditure. Brazil's military spending increased incrementally from 2009 to 2018, leading to a 16.7 rise in 2018.

In 2018, the US administration slightly revamped and disseminated a narrative of renewed 'era of great-power competition'. This was meant to indicate a shift in threat perceptions from insurgencies to large established military powers, notably China, Russia and Iran; it also includes an ambitious arms modernization programme covering both conventional and nuclear capabilities. Participation in wars in the Middle East and increasing tensions with Iran also drive military spending up, although there is less clarity on the costs entailed by direct military involvement in these regions. Mexico has been fighting domestic drug cartels since the mid-2000s, with no resolution in sight, and also struggles with corruption within the police forces, which siphon off available funding. Brazil's military expenditure has grown steadily over a ten-year period. A significant part of the funding goes to military pay and pensions, a heritage from the end of the military dictatorship; another goes to an ambitious arms modernization programme, which is done in cooperation with European companies, such as France Naval Group for the submarine programme. There is no direct defence threat to Brazil's sovereignty and national security, leaving analysts somewhat puzzled as to the need for some of those costly weapons systems (Quéau, 2014). Brazil also led military-style armed operations by raiding the Rio de Janeiro favelas where drug cartels may have been operating (Phillips, 2018).

Asia and Oceania is the only region with uninterrupted growth in military expenditure from 1989 to 2018 (see Figure 1.2), with a total spending of $507 billion.[10] Considering its breadth, Asia and Oceania are divided into four sub-regions: Central and South Asia, East Asia, South-East Asia and Oceania. As it is the case in all regions, one sub-region—East Asia—dominates the regional trend with a military expenditure of $350 billion, a share of 69% of Asia's total.

East Asia's military expenditure's importance is largely due to China, which is the second largest spender in the world after the US. East Asia also includes Japan and South Korea, two other significant spenders in the sub-region with respectively $46.6 billion and $43.1 billion in 2018. Central and South Asia is the second largest spending sub-region with $85.9 billion spending in 2018. Central Asia covers the central Asian republics: Kazakhstan, Kyrgyzstan, Tajikistan, Turkmenistan and Uzbekistan. In 2018, only Kazakhstan and Kyrgyzstan published their military expenditure, with the spending of $1.6 billion and $121.2 million respectively. South Asia's military expenditure, excluding the Central Asia republics, is $84.1 billion in 2018, 98% of the sub-region's military expenditure. This figure is driven by India's military spending, the highest of the sub-region with a spending of

$66.5 billion in 2018. New Delhi's military expenditure increased steadily over the decade, except for small decreases in 2012–2013. The second largest military spender in South Asia is Pakistan, with a more modest figure of $11.4 billion in 2018. South-East Asia is the third sub-region in terms of military spending with a total of $41.9 billion. South-East Asia includes smaller countries such as Cambodia and Myanmar. The largest spending country in the sub-region is Singapore, with a military expenditure of $10.8 billion in 2018, followed by Thailand with $6.8 billion. Finally, Oceania, which covers four countries, displays the smallest figure of military expenditure in the whole region with a total of $29.1 billion. Australia is by far the largest spender in the sub-region with military outlays of $26.7 billion. Oceania's share is 5.7% of regional military expenditure in 2018.

In Central and East Asia, China, the second largest spender with an estimated $250 billion, has been implementing a long-term strategy to become a significant military power. The approach to national security is one that expands China's 'comprehensive national military power' to ensure its status as a major power (Office of the Secretary of Defense, 2019). Notably, it has implemented a strategy to improve its military capabilities by developing large weapons systems such as an aircraft carrier. This plan is largely perceived by countries in the region as a more aggressive posture from Beijing in the Pacific and has raised alarms all over East Asia. For example, Chinese island building (the Spratly Islands and the Paracel Islands) has aggravated sovereignty disputes in the South China Sea that remain unsolved in 2019. In South Asia, the enduring disagreement between India and Pakistan over Kashmir reignited into a war in the same year. Total Pakistani military expenditure is equivalent to 17% of India's military spending. However, both New Delhi and Islamabad have nuclear military capabilities, so an escalation of the conflict, which could potentially involve nuclear capabilities, would have significant impact in the region, and in the world. In 2018, the US decided to pull out of the Joint Comprehensive Plan of Action (JCPOA) for Iran, also called the Iran Deal, which was intended to reduce the stockpile of enriched uranium by Iran, among other things. However, there is little clarity as to why the US withdrew from the Iran Deal.

Europe is the third largest spending region, with a total military expenditure of $364 billion in 2018, a 1.4 increase compared to 2017. The region is split in three sub-regions, Central, Eastern and Western Europe. Central Europe includes 17 countries for which SIPRI has figures. Most of the states in Central Europe are modest spenders, such as the Baltic countries (Estonia $618.9 million, Latvia $679.9 million and Lithuania 1.0 billion), Croatia with $889.5 million or Albania with $180.5 million. The largest military expenditure in the sub-region is Poland's, with a total of $11.6 billion in 2018. Central Europe increased its collective military expenditure by 35% for the 2009–2018 period, bringing the sub-regional total to $28.3 billion. Eastern Europe's military spending is dominated by Russia with $61.4 billion in 2018. This compares to the combined figures of $8.1 billion for the six other East-European countries for which SIPRI has data (Armenia, Azerbaijan, Belarus, Georgia, Moldova and Ukraine). Western Europe, the largest European sub-region expenditure by far, with a total of $266 billion in 2018, includes several of the largest spenders in the world, notably France, which is ranked at the 5th position, the UK at the 7th, followed by Germany at the 8th. Western Europe military expenditure declined over the 2009–2018 decade by 4.9%.

Over the 2009–2018 period, the financial crisis had significant impacts on the largest sub-regional spenders. The UK, for instance, saw a decrease of 16.6% from the high of 2009 to the low of 2015. From 2016 to 2018, shaky growth in the country may indicate another up-cycle as it is planning an arms modernization programme. France shows a similar downward pattern between 2009 and 2013, also due to the financial crisis. However, France's decline represents about half the UK's, with an 8.2% decrease in expenditure for that period. The country returned to growth quickly until the slight reduction of 1.4% in 2018, due to President Macron's decision to stop the transfers of funds from other ministries to the Ministry of Defence to support military operations overseas. France, as is the case in the UK and Germany, is implementing an arms modernization programme and is also involved in armed conflict, notably in the Sahel region. Germany also displays impacts of the financial crisis on its military expenditure. However, Berlin spending contracted slightly, on average by 1.7% from 2011 to 2014. The year 2015 indicates a return to growth in military expenditure until 2018 with an increase of 12.2%, which outpaces the decline. Germany is also engaged in major modernization programmes, notably the development and production of a new generation of combat aircraft, in cooperation with France.

There has been growing wariness towards Russia's intentions in the region, notably from Central European countries and parts of Western Europe. Nordic countries, mainly Sweden and Norway are particularly worried, as they fear growing tensions in the Arctic as well as Russia's military 'build-up'. Stockholm estimates that a European conflict could start in Sweden and has therefore implemented measures to prepare for this contingency by re-instating conscription in 2017 (The Economist, 2018). Norway, which is a member of the Alliance, has worked to convince NATO colleagues, especially the US, to dedicate more military personnel and resources to the Baltic, which led Washington to double the number of US marines present there (Gwadys and Solsvik, 2018). Central European countries are also wary about Russia's intentions in the rest of Europe. Poland especially, feels threatened by Russia which has been described as 'aggressive' by Poland's deputy minister of Foreign Affairs. Following a request from Poland's president, the US deployed 1,000 soldiers in the country, which has increased the tensions between Poland and Russia. Eastern European countries show greater diversity in their relations with Russia. Some countries are at odds with Moscow, such as Georgia over South Ossetia, some are engaged in armed conflicts such as the war with Russia in the Donbass region of Eastern Ukraine since 2014, while others, such as Azerbaijan, maintain cordial relationship despite disagreements between Armenia and Azerbaijan over the Nagorno-Karabakh conflict. Russia has a moderator role in this last issue and strives to maintain the current ceasefire.

The **Middle East** is a difficult region to address due to lack of transparency on military expenditure, and gaps in reporting for countries that present their military spending figures. Data is not available for Syria at all, and three countries do not publicly report their military expenditure in the 2010 decade: Qatar in 2011, Yemen in 2015 and the UAE also in 2015. Because of the absence of too many data points, SIPRI does not provide a regional estimate for the Middle East. For instance, the UAE's military expenditure figures increased by 136% from the low of 2006 to 2014. Knowing that the UAE was still involved in major military operations in Yemen in 2018 and remained militarily involved in Libya, the UAE military expenditure is likely to be much more substantial in 2018 than in 2014. Moreover, the country also acquired large and costly weapons systems, which would also lift the Emirates' spending. Nevertheless, several countries in the region do report their military expenditure. Indeed, it is the case for most of them.

In 2018, data is missing for Qatar, Syria, the UAE and Yemen. Unsurprisingly, the largest spender of the region is Saudi Arabia, which is leading the war against Houthi rebels in Yemen since 2015. In 2018, Riyadh displayed the largest military burden in the world, dedicating 8.8% of its GDP to its military expenditure. The coalition of Middle East countries fighting with Saudi Arabia includes Bahrein, Egypt, Jordan, Kuwait, Qatar and the UAE. Countries in the Saudi coalition for which we have data (Bahrein, Egypt, Jordan, Kuwait) all show increases in their spending from 2015 to 2017 except for Egypt. All decreased their spending in 2018 except for Kuwait. Turkey, the second largest spender in the region has been in an almost uninterrupted armed conflict over Kurdistan's independence starting in 1984, with breaks in hostilities until 2015, when another conflict arose and is still ongoing in 2019. The third largest spender in the region is Israel, with a total spending of $15.9 billion in 2018. Israel is in regular armed conflict with Hamas in Gaza, as well as escalating tensions with Hezbollah in Lebanon – backed by Iran – which tends to drive military spending up.

Relationships between the countries of the Middle East are very tense and complicated within the region, especially between Iran, Saudi Arabia, the UAE and Qatar.[11] Saudi Arabia has called for the US to do a surgical strike in Iran following the announcement that Teheran had breached the nuclear stockpile threshold of enriched uranium agreed in the Iran Deal. It is also implementing an arms modernization programme through imports, which may incite other countries of the region to do the same.

Qatar also has a close commercial relationship with Iran, as they share the largest gas field in the world, which puts the country at odds with Saudi Arabia and the UAE (Hincks, 2019). There seems to be a power struggle over which country will influence the region most. Several of them are also involved in wars, which are, as previously mentioned, important drivers of growth in military expenditure.

1.5 Conclusion

a) *A renewed 'great-power competition': a misleading, biased and dangerous narrative*

Current global and regional trends in military expenditure display an up-cycle driven primarily by arms modernization programmes in several large and medium military powers, as well as wars and to different degrees, threat perceptions. According to SIPRI data, all regions have increased their military expenditure over the 2009–2018 decade except for the Americas, which show a decrease of 17% for the same period. However, following his inauguration in 2017, Trump planned to increase military expenditure significantly. This was also presented along with a narrative of hardening international relations labelled as 'A new era of great-power competition' with Russia and China, which seems to have gained traction in other countries, notably in Central Europe with regard to Russia and in East Asia and Australia in regard to China. NATO, which includes most Western and several Central European countries as well as the US, also looks to have adopted a more assertive stance towards Russia. Moreover, the US-China trade war has made the relationship between the two largest military spenders, which are also the two largest economies, very tense.

The situation described above portrays a hardening of international relations characterized by distrust and competition; it also places national security as the highest state priority. The perception of a challenging and increasingly dangerous security landscape is also partly due to efforts by large arms-producing countries to modernize their arsenals by developing new generations of weapon systems, some of which would incorporate currently emerging technologies such as artificial intelligence, hypervelocity, drone-swarms, quantum radar and space-based weaponry.

There are also plans to modernize nuclear capabilities. Alarmingly, nuclear arsenals are implicitly presented as a significant part of the 'great power competition' and several nuclear countries, notably the US, China, France, Russia and the UK are currently modernizing or planning to update some or all their nuclear capabilities, including delivery systems. These nuclear modernization programmes would include the emerging technologies mentioned above, in order to increase lethality and speed and to counteract defences. Other means of waging warfare, such as cybersecurity and disinformation, are also increasingly discussed and considered as threats, but these are very hard to identify and quantify in terms of their costs and the potential damage they can cause, as they are not often discussed publicly. The costs associated with these projects are unknown, but likely to be extremely high.

All of this underscores that the so-called 'new era of great-power competition' promotes first and foremost military preparedness and responses to what are considered threats, deepening the feeling of insecurity and intensifying tensions. It focusses on the military as the guarantor of national security and de facto relegates some of the most important (in)security issues of the next few years and decades, namely, social inequality, economic volatility and climate change, to the background.

Considering the current international security environment, it is important to promote solutions to limit the military burden on national and global wealth, to preserve societies from the increasing influence of military institutions, to bolster diplomatic capabilities in order to renew bilateral and multilateral strategic dialogue, and to find alternatives to wars at a time when threats such as global warming will have impacts that are not yet well understood on human security.

b) The importance of transparency and rigorous and evidence-based research and analysis

One important element to highlight at the close of the decade is the significant tensions between states, which seems to translate into partial, and sometimes misleading, information on the intentions of other states. This is where transparency and independent research are key: they provide non-partisan, transparent and open-source information alongside diplomatic initiatives. They can also help defuse some security concerns by presenting the rationales for decisions such as the launch of large arms modernization programmes both nuclear and conventional, highlight the impetus for such modernization, clarify motivations for transferring arms to countries at war, as well as participation of third parties in countries engaged in war.

Despite the 'back to the future' feeling that the catchphrase 'a new era of great-power competition' induces for those of us old enough to remember the Cold War, evidence shows that the complicated and volatile 2010 decade (and likely the 2020) is certainly not a belated 'Cold War Sequel'. Presenting it as such is severely misrepresenting the current intertwined political-economic and political-strategic dynamics, which have been deeply transformed through economic globalization, almost universal access to information through internet, arms industry internationalization and climate change. Learning from former tense periods such as the Cold War or the few years before the 1914–1918 War are, without a doubt, instructive. However, they cannot be applied to the contemporary global security landscape without infusing a good dose of distortion.

Notes

1 The authors would like to thank Alexandra Kuimova for reviewing fact-checking and suggesting text for this chapter.

2 All percentage changes use 2017 constant US dollars; percentage shares use 2018 current dollars. Figures are also presented in current 2018 US dollars. All figures are from the SIPRI military expenditure database 2018, unless otherwise specified.
3 The Reagan build-up was a very large increase in US military expenditure in the 1980s, notably to increase military capabilities by developing large weapons systems.
4 SIPRI scrutinizes 168 countries every year for military expenditure information. However, it happens often that data is unavailable for several countries or that figures are too problematic to be included in the SIPRI military expenditure database.
5 The Regional figure for Africa excludes Eritrea and Somalia because of lack of data.
6 There are 54 states in Africa and two countries claiming statehood – Western Sahara and Somaliland. SIPRI has military expenditure estimates for 51 of the African States.
7 SIPRI considers Egypt as a Middle East country, and therefore, it is not included in the Africa estimate.
8 Costs of France's military overseas operations were about 1.3 billion euro in 2018.
9 The regional figure for America excludes Cuba because of lack of data.
10 The regional Asia figure excludes North Korea, Turkmenistan and Uzbekistan.
11 The conflict in Syria, which involves Saudi Arabia and the UAE in Syria; the war in Yemen also involving Saudi Arabia and the UAE; and the Israeli-Palestinian conflict, to name a few.

Bibliography

Congressional Research Service (2019), *Renewed Great Power Competition: Implications for Defense and Issues for Congress*, Report R43838. Available at: https://fas.org/sgp/crs/natsec/R43838.pdf

Gwadys, F., Solsvik, T. (2018), "Russian Buildup Worries Norway before Big NATO Military Exercise". *Reuters World News*, Toronto, 2 October. Available at: https://www.reuters.com/article/us-norway-arctic-nato-russia/russian-buildup-worries-norway-before-big-nato-military-exercise-idUSKCN1MC123

He, L. (2019), "China's Economic Slowdown Is Real, but It's Not Just about Tariffs". *CNN Business*, Atlanta, 19 July. Available at: https://edition.cnn.com/2019/07/19/economy/china-economy-trump-trade-war/index.html

Hincks, J. (2019), "How U.S. Allies in the Middle East are Responding to Rising Tensions with Iran", *Time Magazine*, New York, 18 June. Available at: https://time.com/5608930/pomepo-iran-saudi-uae-tankers/

Nan Tian et al. (2019), "Military Expenditure" in SIPRI Yearbook 2019, Stockholm International Peace Research Institute (SIPRI), Stockholm, Oxford University Press, pp.185–221.

Office of the Secretary of Defense (2019), *Military and Security Developments Involving the People's Republic of China*, Annual report to Congress, 2 May. Available at: https://media.defense.gov/2019/May/02/2002127082/-1/-1/1/2019_CHINA_MILITARY_POWER_REPORT.pdf

Phillips, D. (2018), Brazil Military's Growing Role in Crime Crackdown Fuels Fears among Poor", *The Guardian*, London, 27 Feb. Available at: https://www.theguardian.com/world/2018/feb/27/brazil-military-police-crime-rio-de-janeiro-favelas

Quéau, Y. (2014), *Are the Brazilian Military Industrial Ambitions at Risk?* Multilateral Security Governance Conference, Rio de Janeiro. Published by the Konrad Adenauer Foundation. Available at: academia.edu/9405506/Are_the_Brazilian_Military_Industrial_Ambitions_at_Risk_

Stockholm International Peace Research Institute (SIPRI) (2019), Military Expenditure Database'. Available at: https://www.sipri.org/databases/milex

The Economist (2018), "Russia's Growing Threat to North Europe", *The Economist*, London, 6 October. Available at: https://www.economist.com/europe/2018/10/06/russias-growing-threat-to-north-europe

Wong, E. (2019), "U.S. versus China; A New Era of Great-power Competition, But without Boundaries", *The New York Times*, New York, 6 June. Available at: https://www.nytimes.com/2019/06/26/world/asia/united-states-china-conflict.html

2 Military expenditure, arms transfer and armed conflicts

Chloé Meulewaeter

2.1 Introduction

At the global level there is an increasing trend in military expenditure, arms transfer and armed conflicts. Military spending in 2018 reached a historical record of US$1.8 trillion, while the volume of arms exports has already surpassed two of the three recorded transfer peaks. Last year there were 52 armed conflicts, only one conflict less than the maximum reported. It is urgent to analyse the interrelationship between these processes of militarization of society.

Previous researches have analysed the link between arms transfer and armed conflict. Fauconnet et al. (2018) have analysed the effect of the arms trade on the intensity of intrastate conflicts. They have found that global major and conventional weapons exports have an exacerbating impact on intrastate conflicts. In line with this research, Pamp et al. (2018) have investigated the impact of governments' arms imports on the onset of intrastate conflicts. The authors have found that arms imports significantly increase the probability of an onset of intrastate armed conflicts. Two recent reports of the Centre Delàs for Peace Studies and the School of Culture of Peace (2017, 2018) have investigated European arms exports to countries in tension. The reports provide descriptive data on the countries' importers on arms originating in the European Union and on the main European exporters to countries in tension. On the link between military expenditure and armed conflicts, to the best of our knowledge only one academic paper has specifically investigated how military expenditure relates to internal armed conflicts (Collier and Hoeffler, 2002), with the conclusion that high spending did not appear to deter rebellion. Defence economics literature focusses rather on the economic impact of military spending, be it economic growth or the opportunity cost of military expenditure.

As there is a dearth of theoretical work on this topic, we propose a possible mechanism linking military expenditures to armed conflicts: the economic military cycle (Calvo Rufanges, 2015). It shows how military spending might lead to or facilitate conflicts by illustrating the process of militarization and arms build-up of a society. The military economic cycle establishes that, through the demand that the armed forces puts on the arms industry, military spending is responsible for ensuring that military industries are able to maintain sustained production and supply in arms markets, and therefore, arms are finally used in contexts of armed conflict.

The methodology we use in this work is quantitative analysis with panel data, which captures the time evolution of military expenditure, arms transfer and armed conflict data for all available states. To summarize the data, we present descriptive statistics on global and regional military spending, arms transfers and armed conflicts, with data from the Stockholm International Peace Research Institute (SIPRI) databases on military expenditure and arms transfer, and data from the Uppsala Conflict Data Program (UCDP) database on armed conflict.

The main objective of this research work is to carry out statistical analyses to relate military expenditure and arms transfer to each other and with the intensity of armed conflicts (minor armed conflicts and wars). We aim to assess to what extent military spending leads to an increase in the intensity of armed conflicts, and to assess the linkage of the volume of arms transfers with the escalation of armed conflicts. First, we will see the relationship between military expenditure and arms transfer. Second, we will consider the link between military spending and armed conflicts. And third, we will analyse the relationship between arms transfer and armed conflicts.

In the second section of this chapter we present descriptive data on military expenditure, arms transfers and armed conflicts. In Section 3 we present how these concepts relate to each other according to the main objective of this work. In Section 4 we present conclusions on the relationship between world military expenditures, arms transfers and armed conflicts and we also outline recommendations aimed at building peace. Finally, in the fifth section of this paper we present some limitations of our work and future research perspectives.

2.2 General trends

2.2.1 General trends of military expenditure

SIPRI provides data for military expenditure with consistent time series for the period 1949–2018. Although data availability varies substantially from country to country, data from at least the late 1950s are available for most countries that were independent at the time.

In Figure 2.1 we can observe the evolution of global military spending.[1] We use the military expenditure database (SIPRI, 2019a) that provides information for 173 countries for the period 1949–2018. The variable *military_expenditure* is calculated in million USD, at constant 2017 prices and exchange rates, except for 2018, which is in million USD, at 2018 prices and exchange rates. As we can see, the global trend in military spending has generally

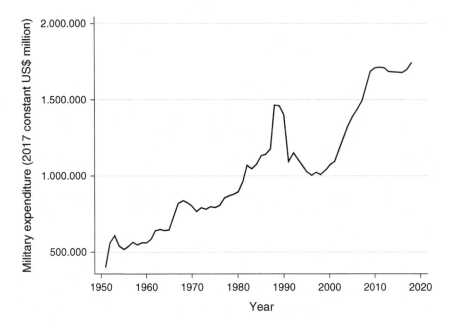

Figure 2.1 World military expenditure, 1949–2018.
Source: own elaboration with data from SIPRI (2019a).

followed an upward trend since 1949. With the exception of the significant drop after the end of the Cold War, world military spending has experienced little reduction in its evolution. At present military expenditure has surpassed the peak prior to the end of the Cold War. The latest available data reveal that world military spending in 2018 reached the all-time record of US$1.8 trillion.

Disparities between regions are considerable. In 2018, the prevalence of the Americas stands out above all other regions of the world, because the United States is the country with by far the highest military spending in the world, with US$649 billion (see Figure 2.2). In fact, the United States defence budget alone exceeds the defence budget of any other region of the world. The Americas' defence budget total is followed in importance by Asia, Europe and the Middle East. Africa and Oceania end the list of regional military powers in 2018.

2.2.2 General trends of arms transfer

SIPRI has developed its own unit to measure the volume of international exports and imports of major conventional weapons, the trend-indicator value (TIV). This unit intends to represent the volume of transfer of military resources rather than sales prices. It relates on actual deliveries of major and

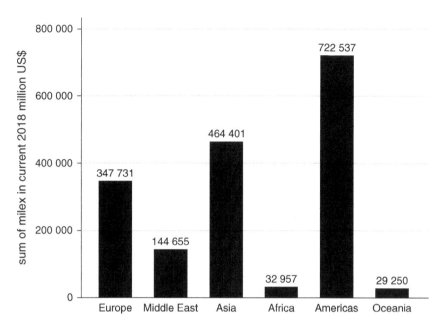

Figure 2.2 Total military expenditure, by region, 2018.
Source: own elaboration with data from SIPRI (2019a).

conventional weapons and it aims to allow for the measurement of general trends to facilitate comparisons over time and countries. In Figure 2.3 we observe the evolution of the volume of global arms exports within the period 1950–2018. The bar graph shows annual totals and the line graph shows the five-year moving average.[2]

As we can see in Figure 2.3, and in accordance to SIPRI latest report on trends on international arms transfers (Wezeman et al., 2019), the volume of international transfer of major and conventional weapons has grown steadily since 2003. While the volume of arms exports has not reached the peak of the last years of the Cold War, the graph shows that the current global trend is a constant increase that has already surpassed two of the three highest levels of global arms exports in History. According to the authors (Wezeman et al., 2019), the main regions of arms importing countries in the period 2014–2018 are Asia and Oceania, followed by the Middle East, Europe, Africa and the Americas. The regions of the five main arms exporting countries for the same period are Americas, Europe and Asia, with the United States being the state that exports more arms with 36% of total exports. The moving average line shows a steady upward trend since 2005.

The level of exports and imports by region, with data from 2018, is shown in Figure 2.4. The blue bars show the average exports by region in million TIV, while the red bars show the average imports by region in million TIV.

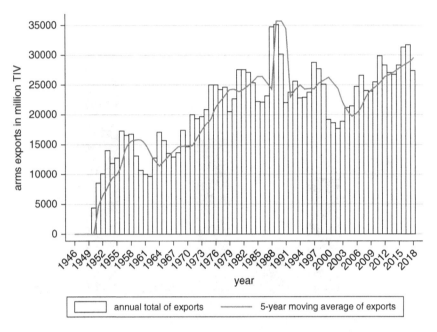

Figure 2.3 Volume of global arms exports, 1950–2018.
Source: own elaboration with data from SIPRI (2019b).

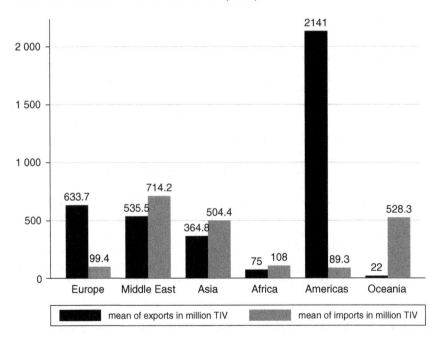

Figure 2.4 Mean of arms exports and imports by region, year 2018.
Source: own elaboration with data from SIPRI (2019b).

Table 2.1 The 15 largest exporters/importers of Major Conventional Weapons, MCW (in million TIV), in 2018

Main exporters	m. TIV	Region	Main importers	m. TIV	Region
1 United States	10508	Americas	1 Saudi Arabia	3810	Middle East
2 Russia	6409	Europe	2 Australia	1572	Oceania
3 France	1768	Europe	3 China	1566	Asia
4 Germany	1277	Europe	4 India	1539	Asia
5 Spain	1188	Europe	5 Egypt	1484	Middle East
6 Korea, South	1083	Asia	6 Algeria	1318	Middle East
7 China	1040	Asia	7 Korea, South	1317	Asia
8 United Kingdom	741	Europe	8 Pakistan	777	Asia
9 Israel	707	Middle East	9 Turkey	685	Middle East
10 Italy	611	Europe	10 Japan	696	Asia
11 Netherlands	369	Europe	11 United States	613	Americas
12 Turkey	363	Middle East	12 Iraq	596	Asia
13 Switzerland	243	Europe	13 Thailand	578	Asia
14 Ukraine	224	Europe	14 Viet Nam	546	Asia
15 South Africa	149	Africa	15 Norway	537	Europe

Source: own elaboration with data from SIPRI (2019b).

Figure 2.4 clearly indicates that the Americas and Europe have much higher levels of arms exports than imports, while the Middle East, Oceania and Asia have a volume of arms imports well above their exports. In Africa, 2018 data show almost equal levels of exports and imports. As these last data are regional averages, Table 2.1 presents a table with the data of the 15 main exporters/importers by country in 2018, in order to display which are the main countries in each category.

2.2.3 General trends of armed conflicts

In our calculation, we use the variable *intensity_level* from the Uppsala Conflict Data Program at the department of Peace and Conflict Research (UCDP/PRIO) armed conflict dataset that refers to the intensity level in the conflict per calendar year and provides data for the period 1946–2018. This variable distinguishes between minor armed conflicts and war, and codes minor conflicts with at least 25 battle-related deaths per year, and wars are observed when battle-related deaths exceed 1,000 battle deaths per year.

The Uppsala Conflict Data Program (UCDP) defines a state-based armed conflict as: "a contested incompatibility that concerns government and/or territory where the use of armed force between two parties, of which at least one is the government of a state, results in at least 25 battle-related deaths in a calendar year" (Pettersson, 2019b). UCDP distinguishes between primary parties and secondary parties. Primary parties are those that form an incompatibility (over government and/or territories) by stating incompatible positions, and secondary parties are states that enter a conflict to support one of the primary parties with troops (Pettersson, 2019b). Among the primary parties, UCDP distinguishes two groups: *side_a* and *side_b*. The *side_a* category always refers to the government of a state, and the *side_b* category refers to the country or actor of the opposition. The *side_b* category might be the government of a state or a military group. In our variable design, we attribute conflicts to countries whose government is in the *side_a* category. The other states involved in the conflicts, whether in the opposition or in the side_b category, are therefore eliminated from the analysis. (For example, in 2018 the UCDP/PRIO Armed Conflict Dataset observed two wars in Afghanistan. In one of them the Government of Afghanistan is *side_a*, while the government of the United States is *side_b* category. For the other war observed that same year in Afghanistan, the government of Afghanistan appears again in the *side_a* category, while the governments of Pakistan and the government of the United States are in the *side_b* category. For that reason, the two conflicts occurring in Afghanistan in 2018 are attributed only to Afghanistan.)

Figure 2.5 shows the evolution of armed conflicts in the period 1946–2018, differentiating between minor conflicts and wars. As we can see, since

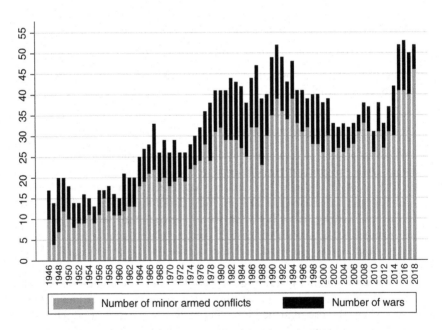

Figure 2.5 World armed conflicts, by intensity level, 1946–2018.
Source: own elaboration with data from UCDP/PRIO Armed Conflict Dataset (Gleditsch et al., 2002; Pettersson et al., 2019a).

the beginning of data collection, there has been a clear upward trend, reaching in 1991, 52 armed conflicts in the world. At the end of the Cold War, the number of armed conflicts in the world decreased until 2003, when the upward trend resumed. Since 2015, we can observe a peak in the number of armed conflicts in the world, which equals or exceeds 50 occurrences. The maximum of 53 armed conflicts was observed in 2016. However, 2018 was the year in which the number of minor armed conflicts reached an historical peak, with a total of 46 cases. Figure 2.5 reports that the historical minimum of minor armed conflicts was in 1947 with four conflicts, and the historical minimum and maximum of wars were, respectively in 1947 with two occurrences and in 1988 with 16.

The number of minor armed conflicts and the number of wars by country in 2018 are shown in Table 2.2. It also shows the region of each conflict. According to Table 2.2, in 2018 there were 20 minor armed conflicts in Africa, 14 in Asia, nine in the Middle East, two in Europe and one in the Americas; and there were three wars in the Middle East, two in Asia and one in Africa.

Table 2.2 Number of armed conflicts in 2018, by country

Country	Minor	Wars	Region	Country	Minor	Wars	Region
Afghanistan	0	2	Asia	Mozambique	1	0	Africa
Algeria	1	0	Africa	Myanmar	3	0	Asia
Burkina Faso	1	0	Africa	Niger	1	0	Africa
Cameroon	1	0	Africa	Nigeria	2	0	Africa
Central African Republic	1	0	Africa	Pakistan	2	0	Asia
				Philippines	3	0	Asia
Chad	2	0	Africa	Russia	1	0	Europe
Colombia	1	0	Americas	Rwanda	1	0	Africa
Congo, Dem. Rep.	1	0	Africa	Somalia	1	1	Africa
				South Sudan	1	0	Africa
Egypt	2	0	Middle East	Sudan	1	0	Africa
India	4	0	Asia	Syria	1	2	Middle East
Indonesia	1	0	Asia				
Iran	3	0	Asia	Thailand	1	0	Asia
Iraq	1	0	Asia	Turkey	1	0	Middle East
Israel	1	0	Middle East				
Kenya	1	0	Africa	Uganda	1	0	Africa
Libya	1	0	Africa	Ukraine	1	0	Europe
Mali	2	0	Africa	Yemen North	0	1	Middle East
Subtotal minor armed conflicts	46			Subtotal wars		6	
Total Armed conflicts 2018	52						

Source: own elaboration with data from UCDP/PRIO Armed Conflict Dataset (Gleditsch et al., 2002; Pettersson et al., 2019a).

2.2.4 Summary of general trends

As descriptive statistics show, there is an increasing trend in military expenditure, arms transfer and armed conflicts. The latest data on military spending shows that it has never been so high in history; the volume of arms exports, illustrated with a moving average, shows a steady upward trend since 2005, and last year was the year in which the number of minor armed conflicts reached an historical peak, with a total of 46 cases.

Descriptive statistics on regional trends show huge disparities between regions. Our descriptive statistics with data of military expenditure in 2018, data of arms transfer in 2017, and data of armed conflicts in 2018 show that the Americas is the region with the highest military spending in the world, its export volume (the highest in the world) is much higher than its import volume and it has the lowest number of armed conflicts in the world. By contrast, Africa is a region with relatively low military spending, the lowest volume of exports and imports and the highest number of armed conflicts in 2018.

2.3 The relationship between military expenditure, arms transfer and armed conflicts

2.3.1 On the link between military expenditure and arms transfer

How does military spending relate to arms exports? To answer this question, we relate data from the military expenditure database from SIPRI and data from the arms transfer database also from SIPRI, within the period 1946–2018. The correlation coefficient of military expenditure and arms exports (0.8639, p-value<0.001) shows a strong positive linear relationship between military expenditure and arms exports over time. This means that as military spending increases, arms exports tend to increase in a similar proportion.

The relationship between global military spending and global arms exports for 2018 is displayed in Figure 2.6. The graph shows a strong positive linear relationship between military expenditure and arms exports in 2018, meaning that the higher the military expenditure, the higher the arms exports. Also, the graph shows how the United States clearly differs from the point cloud by having a military expenditure and a volume of arms exports far above the other states. Russia and China follow the United States, with China having a higher military spending than predicted by the fitted values line, while Russia is below the general trend. After these three states follow a point cloud from which it is almost impossible to distinguish different patterns. For this reason, Figure 2.7 shows the relationship between military expenditure and arms exports by region.

In Figure 2.7 we show the relationship between military expenditure and arms exports at the regional level. The first thing to pay attention to, when looking at Figure 2.7 is that the scales for military spending and arms exports

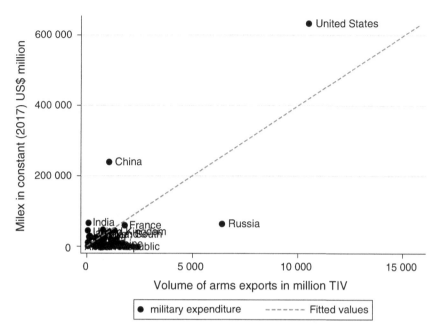

Figure 2.6 Relationship between military expenditure and arms exports, year 2018.
Source: own elaboration with data from SIPRI (2019a) and SIPRI (2019b).

are different for each region. For example, the Americas scale is the largest, given the data from the United States, which differs considerably from all other states on the continent. In Europe, Russia, France, the United Kingdom, Germany, Italy and Spain are the states that stand out from the point cloud due to the size of their military spending and arms exports. Compared to Europe, Asia shows a much smaller scale of arms exports, but a larger scale of military spending, thus showing a different pattern. All in all, the fitted values lines presented in Figure 2.7 all have a positive slope, indicating that the global trend is confirmed at the regional level: the higher the military expenditure, the higher the arms exports. It should be noted, however, that the fitted values line is purely illustrative for Africa, the Middle East and Oceania since there are only two observations per continent. Indeed, as described in Section 2.2., these are mainly importing continents.

2.3.2 On the link between military spending and armed conflicts

We now turn to the relationship between military spending and the intensity of armed conflict. We want to know to what extent the intensity of an armed conflict is related to military expenditure in the year prior to the observation of the conflict. To do so, we have created a lagged variable of military

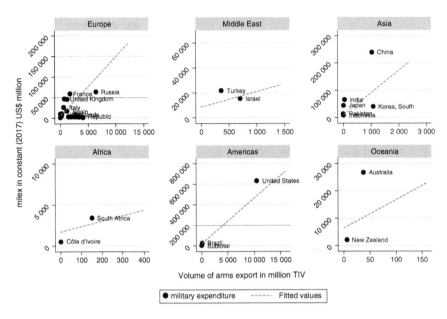

*Figure 2.*7 Relationship between military expenditure and arms exports by region, year 2018.
Source: own elaboration with data from SIPRI (2019a) and SIPRI (2019b).

expenditure. A lagged variable is a variable, which has its value coming from an earlier point in time. In our analysis, the lagged variable of military expenditure is from the year before the observations. This means that the variable shows the average military expenditure of a state in the year before a conflict.

We use the variable *intensity_level* from the UCDP/PRIO Armed Conflict Dataset (Gleditsch et al., 2002; Pettersson et al., 2019a). As the variable provides information only for armed conflicts per country and year, there are no observations when there is no conflict in a country-year. In order to allow for the observation of absence of conflict in a country-year we added a third category that codes 0 if battle-related deaths are below 25. Also, to measure the intensity level of a conflict as a suitable variable to use with panel data, we have created the variable *intensity_level_by_total_deaths*. This variable determines the global intensity of armed conflicts for each country, based on the calculation of the total number of battle-related deaths in each country-year. For example, in 2017 the government of Libya was involved in four minor armed conflicts. The sum of the number of the battle-related deaths from these four conflicts is 404, and therefore, we codify the intensity of the conflicts for Libya in the year 2017 as a minor conflict. In contrast, the government of Sudan was involved in two minor conflicts in 2016, but the sum of the battle-related deaths is 1316. Therefore, in the year 2016 in Sudan we codify a war. This allows us to have only one observation per country-year in order to run panel data analyses, and it allows us to appreciate the general level of intensity of conflicts. The variable *intensity_level_by_total_deaths* is therefore coded as follows:

–0 (absence of conflict) if the battle-related deaths are strictly under 25.
–1 (minor armed conflict) if the battle-related deaths stay between or equal 25 and 999.
–2 (war) if the battle-related deaths equal or exceed 1,000.

In graph 8, we observe that in the case in which a country is not involved in an armed conflict, the previous year its military expenditure was, on average, US$8,532 million. When a government is involved in a minor conflict, on average its military expenditure from the previous year increases to US$24,270 million. However, if it is involved in a war, its military expenditure is more or less equal to the situation of absence of conflict, on average US$8,438 million. An analysis of the variance (ANOVA) shows that the differences in means are statistically significant at 0.1%.

Possibly, the reason why the category *war* is at the same average level as the category *absence of conflict* can be explained by the methodology of the variable design. As noted above, the criterion we use to attribute a conflict to a country, according to the UCDP/PRIO Armed Conflict Dataset, is that the government of that country belongs to *side_a* category. This implies that the United States, which represents the world's largest military expenditure, is found only once in the *war* category (in 2001), while on ten occasions it has been involved in a war, but as an opposition country (*side_b*). In other words, nine observations corresponding to the United States at war are excluded from the analysis. This methodology could underestimate the average military expenditures shown in Figure 2.8. Therefore, due to restrictions on conducting panel data analysis, not all data for all governments engaged in the same conflict can be considered.

To mitigate this effect, we use the average lagged military expenditure as a share of government spending instead of military expenditure in constant 2017 USD, and we calculate how it relates to the intensity of armed conflicts. Military expenditure as a share of government spending provides an indication of the size of the military with respect to the importance of the State. That is, it accounts for the burden of military expenditure with respect to the efforts of a government to provide public goods and services that may, or may not, affect its characterization as a welfare state.

As we can see in Figure 2.9, when a country is at war, its military expenditure as a share of government spending is, on average 13%, and this figure decreases to 11.7% when it is a minor armed conflict and keep decreasing if the country has no event of armed conflict, at the level of 7%. The analysis of the variance (ANOVA) shows that the differences in means are statistically significant at 0.1%. In other words, the increase of the military expenditure as a share of government spending is related to an increase in the intensity level of an armed conflict.

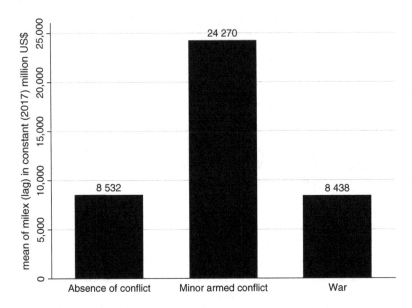

Figure 2.8 Average military expenditure (lag), by conflict intensity level.
Source: own elaboration with data from SIPRI (2019a) and UCDP/PRIO Armed Conflict
Dataset (Gleditsch et al., 2002; Pettersson et al., 2019a).

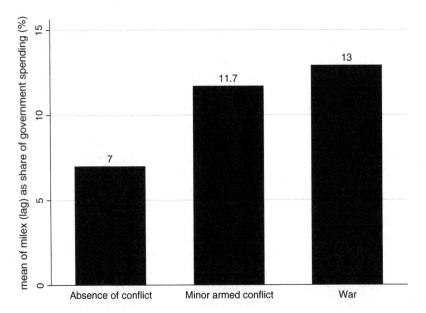

Figure 2.9 Average percentage of military expenditure (lag) as a share of government
spending, by conflict intensity level.
Source: own elaboration with data from SIPRI (2019a) and UCDP/PRIO Armed Conflict
Dataset (Gleditsch et al., 2002; Pettersson et al., 2019a).

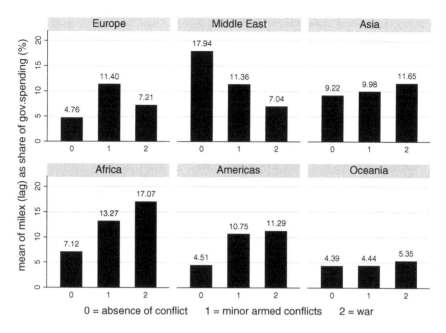

Figure 2.10 Average percentage of military expenditure (lag) as a share of government spending, by conflict intensity level and regions.

Source: own elaboration with data from SIPRI (2019a) and UCDP/PRIO Armed Conflict Dataset (Gleditsch et al., 2002; Pettersson et al., 2019a).

We now proceed to a similar analysis, using regional data. Graph 10 shows how military spending as a share of government spending, in the year prior to the conflict, influences its intensity, at the regional level.

As shown in Figure 2.10, the patterns are significantly different for each continent. In Asia, Africa, Americas and Oceania, the graphs show that the higher the intensity of a conflict, the higher the country's military spending as a share of government spending in the year before the conflict. For example, in Africa, when a country is not involved in any conflict, the previous year its military expenditure as a share of government spending is, on average, 7.12%. When a country's government is engaged in a minor armed conflict, the previous year its military expenditures as a share of government spending is, on average 13.27%, and when an African country is involved in a war, its military expenditures as a share of government spending in the year before the conflict is, on average, 17.07%.

The Middle East shows a totally different pattern, as it seems that military spending as a share of government spending decreases with the increase in the intensity of conflicts. It is possible that this pattern is conditioned by the lack of data since 2014 for Qatar, Syria, the United Arab Emirates and Yemen, as informed in the latest SIPRI report on military expenditure (Tian and et al., 2019).

Europe also shows a different pattern. When the government of a European country is involved in a minor armed conflict or in a war, on average its military expenditure as a share of government spending in the preceding year is higher than in the case where that government is not involved in an armed conflict. However, data show that military spending as a share of government spending is lower in the war category than in the minor armed conflict category.

2.3.3 On the link between arms transfer and armed conflicts

Finally, we assess how arms imports and the intensity of armed conflicts are related. To do this, we use SIPRI data for arms imports (2019b), and UCDP/PRIO Armed Conflict Dataset data for conflict intensity (Gleditsch et al., 2002; Pettersson et al., 2019a). As we do in the previous section, we transform the variable *arms_import* into a lagged variable. In our analysis, the lagged variable of arms import is again from the year before the observations. This means that the variable shows the average arms imports by a state in the year before a conflict. To measure armed conflicts, we use the variable *intensity_level_by_total_deaths*. In that way, we can see the average arms imports of the government of a state, the year before the conflict.

As depicted in Figure 2.11, the average volume of arms imports from a government increases according to the intensity of the conflicts. The states

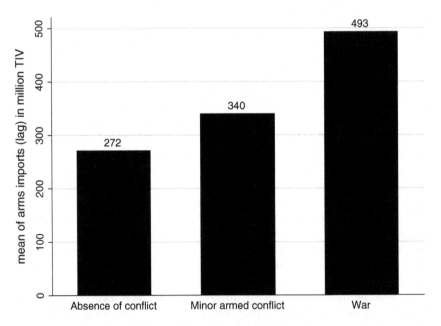

Figure 2.11 Average arms imports of the previous year of the conflict, by conflict intensity level.

Source: own elaboration with data from SIPRI (2019b) and UCDP/PRIO Armed Conflict Dataset (Gleditsch et al., 2002; Pettersson et al., 2019a).

that are not involved in a conflict in a given year import weapons in the previous year per 272 million TIV on average. This figure rises to 340 million TIV if the government is engaged in a minor conflict, rising to 493 million TIV when it is at war. The analysis of variance (ANOVA) shows that there are statistically significant differences between the mean of the groups at 0.1%. In other words, the intensity level of the conflict in which a government is involved is associated with a greater volume of arms imports.

We now conduct a similar analysis at the regional level. Figure 2.12 shows how the volume of arms imports, in the year before the conflict, affects its intensity.

Data at the regional level show different patterns. Looking at the main arms importing continents, as mentioned in Section 2.2., the Middle East, Asia and Oceania, there is a clear difference between the volume of imports in the absence of conflict and the volume of imports in the event of war. The average volume of arms imports of the countries of these continents is higher in the event of war than in the absence of conflict. In the event of a minor armed conflict, the pattern of the data fluctuates. Data from Africa and the Americas show rather similar patterns, which is an increase in the volume of arms imports from the *absence of conflict* category to the *minor armed conflict* category, and a decrease from the *minor armed conflict* to the *war* category.

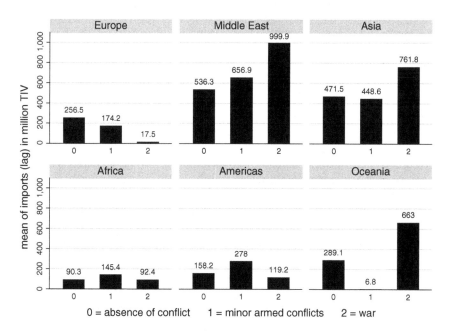

Figure 2.12 Average arms imports of the previous year of the conflict, by conflict intensity level and regions.

Source: own elaboration with data from SIPRI (2019b) and UCDP/PRIO Armed Conflict Dataset (Gleditsch et al., 2002; Pettersson et al., 2019a).

Europe also shows a different pattern, which is a decrease in the volume of arms imports from the absence of conflict to war.

These different patterns can probably be explained by the fact that Europe and the Americas are mainly exporting and not importing continents, and therefore do not display the same behaviour as the mainly importing continents. As mentioned above, Africa has a relatively low level of arms import and export volumes, which may not provide a large amount of data for reliable analysis.

2.4 Conclusion

Our study aims to shed new light on the link between military expenditure, arms transfer and armed conflicts. To put the data in context we provide descriptive statistics to synthesize the general and current trends of military expenditure, arms transfer and armed conflicts, at the global and regional level. Then we turn to our main objective, that is to relate military expenditure and arms transfer, to assess to what extent military spending leads to an increase in the intensity of armed conflicts, and to evaluate the linkage of the volume of arms transfers with the escalation of armed conflicts.

There are three main findings related to our main objective. First, the correlation coefficient of global military expenditure and arms exports shows a strong positive relationship over time. This means that, as military spending increases, arms exports tend to increase in a similar proportion. This conclusion holds at the global and regional level. Second, statistical analysis on military expenditure and the intensity level of the conflicts shows that, at the global level, increases in the intensity level of a conflict are related to a greater military expenditure as a share of government spending in the year previous to the conflict. That is, the more a government spends on the military, the greater the intensity of the conflict in which it is involved. At the regional level, the patterns are different. In Asia, Africa, Americas and Oceania, the graphs are in line with those of the global level. In the Middle East military spending as a share of government spending decreases with the increase in the intensity of conflicts, while in Europe there is an increase from the category *absence of conflict* to the category *minor armed conflict*, and a decrease from the category *minor armed conflict* to *war*. Finally, the intensity level of the conflict in which a government is involved is associated with a greater volume of arms imports the year previous to the conflict. This finding holds at the global level, and it presents variations at the regional level. The average volume of arms imports of the countries of the main importing continents, that is the Middle East, Asia and Oceania, is higher in the event of war than in the absence of conflict. Americas, Africa and Europe show a different pattern.

These empirical findings are consistent with the theory of the military economic cycle (Calvo Rufanges, 2015), which argues that military expenditures and arms transfers are stages in the militarization process of a society, which lead to, or facilitate armed conflict. All in all, our data show a strong relationship between military expenditures, arms transfer and armed conflicts, and therefore we believe that reducing military expenditures and arms exports would allow to lessen the use of military force in conflicts.

2.4.1 Limitations and future research

These results are in line with the military economic cycle theory, but the analysis is not free from limitations, for several reasons. First, due to our variable design, as mentioned above, some data had to be excluded from the analysis. Thus, our results must be nuance, and it should be remembered that they hold for the definition used in the study. The second limitation of our work is related to the nature of the arms transfer data used. Indeed, SIPRI provides data for major and conventional weapons, but not for small arms and lights weapons. However, we believe that many battle-related deaths are the result of the use of small arms and light weapons, not of major conventional weapons. This could explain why, at the descriptive level, Africa's data shows that military spending and arms transfers are low, while it is the region with the most armed conflicts. Unfortunately, we do not have reliable data on small arms and light weapons. A third limitation of our work is that we cannot provide a viable explanation for certain differences in analytical results at the regional level. Therefore, further research to explain these findings is needed.

Nevertheless, the robustness of our results is strong, and we believe the limitations mentioned above inspire future research without compromising the empirical analysis. Indeed, our work raises relevant questions. Do increases in the militarization of a country perpetuate conflicts? Do increases in the militarization of a country lead to new armed conflicts? Also, we only looked at major conventional weapons because of the availability of the data. Thus, what role do small arms and light weapons play in the onset of conflicts and in the intensity level and perpetuation of on-going conflicts? Are there any differences between regions? Providing answers to these questions would bring us a step closer to fully understanding the role of militarization in armed conflict.

Notes

1 The SIPRI definition of military expenditure includes all spending on current military forces and activities, and includes spending on: the armed forces, including peace keeping forces; defence ministries and other government agencies engaged in defence projects; paramilitary forces when judged to be trained, equipped and available for military operations; and military space activities (SIPRI, 2019a).

2 A moving average is a series of average values of different subsets of the full dataset (in our graph each data point in the line graph represents an average for the preceding five-year period). It smooths out the noise of random outliers and emphasizes long-term trends.

Bibliography

Calvo Rufanges, J. (2015), "El ciclo económico militar", in Calvo Rufanges, J. and Pozo Marín, A. (eds) *Diccionario de la paz, la guerra y el desarme*. Barcelona: Icaria, 81–84.

Centre Delàs for Peace Studies and School for a Culture of Peace (2017). *The Arms Trade and Armed Conflicts. An Analysis of European Weapons Exports to Countries in Armed Conflict*. Available at: http://www.centredelas.org/images/INFORMES_i_altres_PDF/Informe_ComerçArmesConflictes_web_ANG_DEFok.pdf

Centre Delàs for Peace Studies and School for a Culture of Peace (2018). *The Arms Trade and Conflict. An Analysis of European Weapons Exports to Countries in Situation of Tension*. Available at: http://www.centredelas.org/images/INFORMES_i_altres_PDF/Informe_ComerçArmesTensio_web_ENG.pdf

Collier, P., and Hoeffler, A. (2002), *Regional Military Spillovers*. Mimeo. World Bank, Washington, DC.

Fauconnet, C., Malizard, J., and Pietri, A. (2018), French Arms Exports and Intrastate Conflicts: An Empirical Investigation. *Journal of Defense and Peace Economics*, 30(2): 176–196.

Gleditsch, N.P., Wallensteen, P., Eriksson, M., Sollenberg, M., and Strand H. (2002), Armed Conflict 1946–2001: A New Dataset. *Journal of Peace Research*, 39(5): 615–637.

Pamp, O., Rudolph, F., Thurner, P.W., Mehltretter, A., and Primus, S. (2018), The Build-up of Coercive Capacities: Arms Imports and the Outbreak of Violent Intrastate Conflicts. *Journal of Peace Research*, 55(4): 430–444.

Pettersson, T., Högbladh, S., and Öberg, M. (2019a), Organized Violence, 1989–2018 and Peace Agreements. *Journal of Peace Research*, 56(4).

Pettersson, T. (2019b), UCDP/PRIO Armed Conflict Dataset Codebook v 19.1. Available at: https://ucdp.uu.se/downloads/

SIPRI (2019a), SIPRI Military Expenditure Database. Available at: https://www.sipri.org/databases/milex

SIPRI (2019b), SIPRI Arms Transfer Database. Available at: https://www.sipri.org/databases/armstransfers

Tian, N., Fleurant, A., Kuimova, A., Wezemanm P. D., and Wezeman, S. T. (2019), *Trends in World Military Expenditure, 2018*. SIPRI, Stockholm.

Wezeman, P. D., Fleurant A., Kuimova, A., Tian, N., and Wezeman, S. T. (2019), *Trends in International Arms Transfer, 2018*. SIPRI, Stockholm.

3 Military spending, foreign military operations and counter-terrorism

Alejandro Pozo Marín

3.1 Introduction

Foreign military operations generally represent a small percentage of military spending. In the case of France, these operations barely accounted for 2.55% of its military spending in 2017, while Spain dedicated 5.6%. For the USA, the "cost of war" accounted for 14% of the Department of Defence spending (Bridey, 2018: 27; Ortega, Bohigas and Mojal, 2017: 21; SIPRI, 2019; US Department of Defence, 2018: 7). However, these operations are one of the most accepted and applauded facets of armed forces and are the topic of many news, images and speeches related to armed forces. It is, therefore, one of its pillars, perhaps the most important from the communicative point of view.

This chapter will analyse the relationship between military spending and foreign military operations. First, it argues that, while the general military spending of some countries has increased since the beginning of this century – despite the economic crisis – the cost of foreign operations has increased to a much greater extent, even multiplied. These missions would have contributed not only with their economic volume, but also as a legitimizing factor of the whole military expenditure. Second, it argues that the bulk of the economic effort of these operations abroad is related to counter-terrorism frameworks and narratives. Three cases will be used: the USA, France[1] and Spain, three NATO member countries with disparate budgetary and interventionist logics.[2]

The Atlantic Alliance requires its members to dedicate at least 2% of their GDP to military spending (NATO, 2019: 3). However, the criteria to calculate this expenditure are not homogenous. For example, the *Gendarmerie* was included in the French Defence budget prior to 2009, and Greece considers as military spending the pensions for its armed forces. However, in Spain the cost of the *Guardia Civil* (a militarized force, like its French counterpart)[3] is under the Ministry of Interior and military pensions are not assumed by the Ministry of Defence. On the contrary, the Ministry of Foreign Affairs and International Development is responsible for the French financial contribution to UN peacekeeping operations (Cour des Comptes, 2016: 8). The NATO criteria, however, include all these components.[4] In any case, the

USA tops the list of military spending among NATO countries and also the percentage with respect to GDP, while France's spending is just below the 2% threshold. Spain would approach the threshold if this country would compute all military items, as NATO recommends, but the budget assigned to the Ministry of Defence falls far short of 2%. However, the Spanish government has argued that its participation in foreign military operations is a much more representative indicator of the country's involvement in global security (Sánchez and Abellán, 2019).

3.2 Military spending increases, but the costs of foreign military operations skyrocket

In 2017, the USA, France and Spain ranked respectively 1st, 6th and 16th in the world list of military spending (SIPRI, 2019). Between 2000 and 2017 the US military spending increased by 41% (peaking in 2010 at nearly 83%) and that of France by 16%, while Spain reduced it by 11% (it came to increase by 5% in 2007) (SIPRI, 2019). It is worth highlighting here that in all three cases there are significant differences regarding how the expenditure is computed and also between the official budget declared and the final actual military expenditure.

However, the costs associated with foreign military interventions have skyrocketed. In France, operations abroad ("Opex") in 2001 cost 604 million euros (Giraud, 2017: 22), while in 2017 they totalled 1,542.4 million (Bridey, 2018: 27), or 2.55 times higher. In Spain, this expenditure increased from 239.63 million euros in 2000 to 1,062.53 million in 2017 (Ortega, Bohigas and Mojal, 2017: 21), or 443%. In the USA, the 9/11 terrorist attacks led to a huge growth in the cost of foreign operations. In fact, the cost in current annual dollars of the War on Terror (including Afghanistan, Iraq and other related operations) is higher than the combined cost of all US wars in the 20th century. In constant dollars of 2011, it is higher than the combined expenditure of the four most significant US wars of that century except for the Second World War: the First World War, Korea War, Vietnam War and the Gulf War (Daggett, 2010: 2). As for the Second World War, with a constant-dollar-of-2011 cost of $4,104 billion, it would be even lower than the estimation made by Brown University, which set the costs of the War on Terror at $4,792 billion up to 2017, including the related "future obligations for veterans medical and disability" until 2053 (Crawford, 2016: 3). However, using a similar methodology – fairer in terms of real spending – the cost of the Second World War would be much higher. The non-base funding used for operations abroad (see below) can be used as an indicator of the evolution of the cost of these operations. While this additional funding accounted for about 2% of the total expenditure of the Ministry of Defence between 1970 and 2000, it represented about 20% on average between 2001 and 2018, peaking at 28% in 2007 and 2008 (Crawford, 2016: 1).

3.3 Foreign military operations in scenarios of counter-terrorism

There are many types of military operations abroad. The three countries analysed in this chapter can do it within the framework of the UN, NATO, the European Union (EU), through coalitions or unilaterally. However, these three countries avoid the UN and prefer other forms of action allowing them more flexibility and more direct satisfaction of their own interests. As of 31 July 2019, the USA did not have any troops on UN missions, while France and Spain had only deployed blue helmet troops in a single scenario: in Lebanon, with United Nations Interim Force In Lebanon (UNIFIL).[5] No UN mission prioritizes uniquely the fight against terrorism. While this is a global concern that also affects the UN, these types of operations are carried out through NATO, in coalitions or unilaterally, often with the collaboration of allied countries. The USA and France stand out for their prioritization of the fight against terrorism in their operations abroad. In the case of Spain, the antiterrorist agenda is combined with the support to ally countries, a constant in the most expensive operations, such as Afghanistan and Iraq (supporting the USA), Lebanon (supporting Israel) or Mali and Central African Republic (supporting France).

In the USA, a large majority of military operations since 9/11 have related to fighting terrorism.[6] The exceptions would be limited to interventions to rescue US citizens elsewhere, the protection of embassies, the war in Libya in 2011, piracy in Somalia, the LRA in Uganda, the crises with North Korea and Iran and actions in Syria or its neighbouring countries. As a whole, the costs associated with these exceptions are very small compared to counter-terrorism missions and, in fact, the various official documents in the USA on the costs of war focus on the latter.

In France, more than 85% of soldiers in missions tagged "military operations abroad" ("*opex*") by the Ministry of Defence are deployed in three contexts with an eminently counter-terrorism objective (in the Sahel, Syria and Iraq) (Ministry of Defence of France, 2019). The French *Cour des Comptes* (Court of Audit)[7] itself catalogues the "nature" of these military operations as "fight against terrorism", and this has also been the case with operations Serval (in Mali), OEF/Heracles (in the Indian Ocean) and FIAS/Pamir (in Afghanistan). However, other missions with other functions could also be located in a context of the fight against terrorism, such as those carried out in Mali, Niger, Djibouti or the Indian Ocean (*Cour des Comptes*, 2016: 16). In 2017, interventions classified as fighting against terrorism totalled 88.5% of the total cost of French military operations abroad (Sénat of France, n.d.).

The case of Spain is more diverse. The only operations with an express counter-terrorism mandate, according to the Ministry of Defence website, are the fight against the Islamic State in Iraq and the support to France in Mali, totalling 609 soldiers in early 2019, or 24%. However, the struggle against terrorism is an important component in Afghanistan, Somalia or Mali, contexts to which Spain devotes a further 483 troops, or another 19% (Ministry of Defence of Spain, 2019).

3.4 Lack of budget transparency for foreign military operations

A common phenomenon in the three countries analysed, while it also applies to others, is to extraordinarily underestimate on purpose the cost of foreign military operations in the budget allocation. As reported by Ortega, Bohigas and Mojal (2017: 21), the Spanish initial annual budget for military operations abroad was 0 euros between 1990 and 1999; 60.10 million euros between 2000 and 2004; 18.36 million in 2005 and 2006; 17.36 million the following two years and 14.36 million between 2009 and 2017, totalling, in 28 years, 501.18 million. The actual final expenditure, however, was, in that same period, of 12,365.68 million euros, almost 25 times higher. In 2017, for example, the Spanish government budgeted 14.36 million and spent 1,062.53, or 74 times, a huge difference compensated every year by the so-called "contingency funds". Although deviations in the final expenditure are understandable due to the uncertainty of what will happen in unstable contexts, these forecasts would be unfeasible even in the case of total withdrawal from all places (due to the cost of the withdrawal itself).

In France, the budget for operations abroad increased progressively from 23 million euros in 2003 to 570 in 2010,[8] and was of 630 million between 2011 and 2013, and 450 between 2014 and 2017, a total of 5,911 million in 15 years, or 394 on average. The actual cost of these operations has been much higher: between 528 and 663 between 2003 and 2006, close to 850 million in 2008, 2009, 2010 and 2012 and between 1,140 and 1,542 in 2011 and between 2013 and 2017 (Bridey, 2018: 27).[9] They totalled 14,260, or 951 on average per year, 2.4 times higher than what was budgeted. The French *Cour des Comptes* alerted in 2016 about the extreme underestimation of these operations, which it considered "insufficiently budgeted and poorly evaluated" (*Cour des Comptes*, 2016: 7). It recommended making a "sincere and realistic forecast of OPEX expenses" and noted that the French State had the capacity to do so, with the exception of an unforeseen crisis (7–8).

In the USA, the Department of Defence has regularly requested and received large extra funding to augment the base-budget funding since 2001. These additional requests are called "nonbase funding", and it has totalled about $2.2 trillion from 2001 to 2018, amounting to about 20% of total defence appropriations. About 98% of the nonbase funding has been used to support activities and operations designated for either overseas contingency operations or what has been deemed the Global War on Terrorism, in Iraq, Afghanistan and elsewhere (Woodward, 2018: 1 and 3). According to a report by the Congressional Budget Office, as mentioned above between 1970 and 2000, nonbase funding accounted for about 2% of the

Department of Defence's total spending. However, from 2001 to 2018, it has averaged about $116 billion per year (in 2019 dollars), or about 20% of the total funding of the Department, and peaking at 28% in 2007 and 2008 (Woodward, 2018: 1). Nonbase funding is generally justified as uncertain and temporary, and it is thus omitted from the Department of Defence's estimates of future defence costs. However, overseas contingency operations funding "has increasingly been used to support enduring activities, including activities that would normally be funded in the base budget". From 2006 to 2018, the Congressional Budget Office has estimated that more than $50 billion in overseas contingency operations funding per year (in 2019 dollars), on average, "has been used to support enduring activities rather than the temporary costs of overseas operations" (Woodward, 2018: 1). The Office identifies two consequences:

> First, the enduring cost of defense programs can be obscured when OCO [(overseas contingency operations)] funding is used to support activities that would be required even if contingency operations ceased. Second, contingency operations can lead to increases in base-budget spending on activities that are not directly related to war or might otherwise not have been funded, creating inaccurate expectations about future funding needs.
>
> (Woodward, 2018: 11)

3.5 Militarist tendency to address political crises

There are different unilateral and collective options to cope with a political crisis abroad, including not only military intervention but also primarily political, diplomatic or economic cooperation. For instance, one of these options may consist of persuading the responsible actors to change their attitudes and promote more peaceful relations. However, in many of the contexts in which their armed forces have acted, the three countries analysed have prioritized a response that is deemed here as heavily militarized.

The USA is, by far, the most paradigmatic example. The two most important sets of foreign military operations of the 21st century have been carried out in Afghanistan and Iraq. In every year between 2001 and 2017, the enormous US official military spending in Afghanistan has multiplied the value of the country's GDP. In 2001, the USA spent 9.1 billion dollars in Afghanistan, 3.6 times the country's GDP of 2.5 billion. Ten years later, while GDP multiplied to over 20 billion, the military cost to the USA reached 97 billion (4.8 times or more than $3,200 per inhabitant of the country in 2011). In total, between 2001 and 2017 the USA spent more than 700 billion dollars militarily,[10] apart from US "aid" that includes not only development cooperation and humanitarian assistance, but also security support-aid totalling 5.1 billion dollars in 2016 alone including 3.7 billion in security aid (Bearak and Gamio, 2016). However, other sources estimate that the total cost in

Afghanistan until 2016 is around two billion dollars (Crawford, 2016), a figure over one hundred times the Afghanistan's GDP in 2017.

In Iraq, a country with a much higher GDP than Afghanistan, in many years the cost of US military operations exceeded its GDP. In 2004[11] the Iraqi GDP was 36.3 billion and the US military spent in Iraq 55 billion. The military spending for the USA in Iraq continued to outpace that country's GDP until 2008,[12] and in the decade between 2003 and 2012, the USA allocated a total of 682 billion dollars. However, other analyses which also include the related future cost provide much higher figures. For example, the aforementioned study estimated the overall cost of operations in Iraq and Afghanistan (including related operations in Pakistan) at 4.79 trillion (Crawford, 2016), more than 30 times the average joint GDP of both countries. It is worth mentioning that many US-allied countries also spent billions of dollars in both Afghanistan and Iraq.[13]

Democratic states are in theory accountable for the consequences of any resort to armed violence against a foreign country. This is particularly needed in two senses: the new situation produced and the damage inflicted on civilians. Tzvetan Todorov (2012) pointed out that NATO's announcement of "irrevocable withdrawal" from Afghanistan for 2014 would be presented as a political success. Although this withdrawal never materialized – NATO continues there – the USA and allies have argued that social and economic indicators have improved significantly in the country. Considering that only a tiny proportion of the world's economic effort in Afghanistan went to non-military-related matters, one may wonder whether that improvement would not be dramatically higher if the bulk of that very same economic effort was committed to political, economic and social developments. But in both countries arms proliferate and a significant part of the responsibility for the situation of violence produced is attributable to the USA. In the 2014–2018 period, Iraq and Afghanistan ranked 8th and 33rd in the list of world arms importers, and 47% of weapons supplied to Iraq and 66% of arms that officially arrived in Afghanistan were exported by the USA (Wezeman et al., 2019: 6). Moreover, according to a project led by Iain Overton, executive director of Action on Armed Violence, the Pentagon has supplied a minimum of 1.45 million firearms to various armed forces and groups in Afghanistan and Iraq, "including more than 978,000 assault rifles, 266,000 pistols and almost 112,000 machine guns" (Chivers, 2016). The actual figure is probably much higher, as, for example, stockpile caches – some by the Islamic State – are not accounted for. The Pentagon is unaware of where many of these weapons have gone, given the levels of desertion and corruption in both countries, among other reasons (Chivers, 2016).

In at least two other military operations, Iraq and Libya, no one dares to claim an improvement in the welfare of the general population as compared to the times when dictators Saddam Hussein and Muammar Gaddafi respectively ruled. In both countries, insecurity and social indicators are worse today than before the respective wars and the death toll among the civilian population has been monstrous. The USA and Spain in Iraq, and both along with France in Libya have contributed to it. However, nobody has been held accountable. On its website, the Spanish Ministry of Defence still justified in September 2019 its intervention in Iraq in 2003 as "humanitarian", while the operation in Libya did not even appear in the list of concluded missions. As for France, Todorov (2012) pointed out that the main promoter in that country of the intervention in Libya, Alain Juppé, former Minister of Defence and Foreign Affairs declared by leaving his post that he was "proud of what we did in Libya".

In Afghanistan, the Spanish political, diplomatic or economic involvements were non-existent prior to the deployment of troops. After the military contribution, they were very small compared to the military effort. For instance, more than nine out of ten Spanish euros for Afghanistan by 2007 were strictly military, and most of the remainder had an important military aim (the improvement of its own security through local acceptance) and was even implemented by the Spanish armed forces (Pozo Marín, 2008: 20). However, the percentage attributable to political participation and diplomacy has been extremely low as compared to the military effort. On the other hand, more than three quarters of the Spanish involvement in Somalia and its related immediate environment at least up to 2008 were strictly military (Martin, De Fortuny and Bohigas, 2012: 51). Another element of concern relates to the fact that Spain has exported "defence materiel", of dual-use or light weapons to governments of the same countries where it deployed troops. For example, 85 million euros in defence materiel to Iraq in 2015, plus another 52 million in 2016 and 33.3 in 2017, the latter two transfers consisting of munitions (González, 2018); more than 11 million euros in defence materiel for Libya in 2010 (the year before the military intervention) or almost two million euros in light weapons since the fall of Gaddafi; almost three million euros in defence materiel exported to Afghanistan between 2013 and 2015; 6.7 million euros in small arms to Lebanon since 2006; or 3.4 million euros in small arms to Central African Republic between 2006 and 2013, the year in which the ongoing armed conflict started (Font and Melero, 2016: 23–42).

In the case of France, according to the Stockholm International Peace Research Institute (SIPRI) database between 2012 and 2018, Paris has not stood out as an arms exporter in any of the countries in which it carries out its two most important operations (with the exception of Senegal, with 32% of total imports coming from France and 8% of the imports to Mali – Spain was responsible for 13% in the latter country). Nor has France stood out, for example, as a donor of humanitarian action. According to the Financial Tracking Service of the UN Office for the Coordination of Humanitarian Affairs (OCHA, 2019), between 2012 and 2018 France contributed an annual average of 3.5 million dollars to Mali, 8.8 million per year to Niger or 9.3 million to Iraq.

3.6 Conclusion

The world's military spending has steadily increased from the 9/11 2001 terrorist attacks in the USA to the present day. This has also been the case in two of the countries analysed, France and the USA, while in Spain the reduction can be explained by the global and internal economic crises that have occurred within that period. However, the costs of military operations abroad have increased in all three cases, contributing not only in terms of economic volume, but also as a legitimizing factor for overall military spending. The bulk of this increase has been developed in scenarios of counter-terrorism, while explanations in the Spanish case are more plural. Likewise, in the three countries there has been a significant lack of budgetary transparency when reporting the cost of military operations abroad. All three drastically underestimate costs in the budget allocation on purpose and have mechanisms to address the surplus: the overseas contingency operations in the USA, the *"surcoûts"* (supplements) in France and the "contingency funds" in Spain. This way, these countries can cover cost overruns that were evidently known in advance, declaring a military spending significantly lower than the one expected.

All three countries, and most prominently the USA, have dedicated a spectacular amount of money to make war. Washington allocated more money to military means in Afghanistan and Iraq than all the goods and services that these countries had. However, both are still mired in violence, as is also the case for most of the countries where these three countries have conducted their main foreign military operations: Pakistan, Mali, Libya, Somalia, Syria and Central African Republic.

The efficiency of military operations is not measured through indicators of medical or humanitarian conditions or economic welfare, but in terms of geopolitical competition. The narratives of foreign military operations are often neither sincere nor honest as per their motivations, objectives and results; they are sometimes conducted with impunity in violation of international law, including acts of aggression (as in Afghanistan and Iraq, and earlier in Kosovo); and warmongers have defended as humanitarian actions of very different nature and intent.

Armed force is not used as last resort. Both total neglect and military intervention cause harm, and there are in between a number of less damaging options to cope with political problems and crises. Unfortunately, without military spending further economic effort has proved rare. There is a need to challenge the manner in which geopolitics plays out within international relations, as well as to question the role of the armed forces in the competition between nations. We need to ask who benefits from foreign intervention (and who is hurt) and what the motives are behind it.

Notes

1 The so-called "Foreign Operations" ("Opex"). Other missions will not be considered, including the deployment in national territory, the so-called "sovereignty

forces" in French overseas territories, naval operations or permanent contingents deployed in some former colonies.

2 The UK is said to present similar figures to those in France (Cour des Comptes, 2016: 20).

3 In 2009 the budget and the staff management of the *Gendarmerie* were attached to the French Ministry of the Interior. Both the *Gendarmerie nationale* and the *Guardia Civil* or the Italian *Carabinieri* (as its French counterpart, one of the four armed forces of the country) are, according to NATO criteria, armed forces and security forces with military status. While they generally provide police functions, they also carry out activities related to threats to their respective countries (such as counter-terrorism) and can be deployed in military missions abroad.

4 The SIPRI military expenditure data may include all current and capital expenditure on: (a) the armed forces, including peacekeeping forces; (b) defence ministries and other government agencies engaged in defence projects; (c) paramilitary forces, when judged to be trained and equipped for military operations; and (d) military space activities. This should include expenditure on: personnel (including salaries of military and civil personnel, retirement pensions of military personnel, and social services for personnel); operations and maintenance; procurement; military research and development; military infrastructure spending, including military bases and military aid (in the military expenditure of the donor country). See https://www.sipri.org/databases/milex/sources-and -methods#definition-of-military-expenditure. Interestingly, NATO's definition of military spending is, in general, similar to SIPRI's (NATO, 2019: 15–16).

5 The USA had deployed a total of 34 people on UN missions, but no troops: 26 were staff officers, four police officers and four experts on seven missions. In addition to the 658 French troops in UNIFIL, France also had 57 staff officers, 26 police officers and two experts in five missions. Apart from 618 troops in UNIFIL, Spain also had 13 staff officers, four experts and 11 police officers in five missions. See https://peacekeeping.un.org/en/troop-and-police-contributors.

6 This includes operations in Afghanistan, Pakistan, Iraq, Yemen, Syria, the Philippines, Djibouti, Somalia, Libya or Mali.

7 In its own description, "the Cour des comptes is the supreme body for auditing the use of public funds in France". See https://www.ccomptes.fr/en/who-we-are -and-what-we-do/cour-des-comptes.

8 Twenty-three million euros in 2003 and 2004; 100 in 2005; 175 in 2006; 360 in 2007; 460 in 2008; 510 in 2009 and 570 in 2010.

9 Six hundred twenty-nine in 2003, 605 in 2004, 528 in 2005, 579 in 2006, 663 in 2007, 831 in 2008, 870 in 2009, 860 in 2010, 1246 in 2011, 873 in 2012, 1257 in 2013, 1140 in 2014, 1293 in 2015, 1344 in 2016 and 1542 in 2017.

10 According to the World Bank, the official GDP of Afghanistan between 2001 and 2017 was, respectively, 2.5, 4.1, 4.6, 5.3, 6.3, 7, 9.8, 10.2, 12.5, 15.9, 17.9, 20.5, 20.3, 20.6, 19.2, 19.5 and 20.8 billion dollars. According to the US Department of Defence (2019: 12), the cost of US military operations in Afghanistan was, also respectively, 9, 11, 13, 10, 14, 14, 25, 31, 48, 83, 97, 90, 75, 60, 45, 38 and 39 billion dollars. However, other sources estimate higher amounts (Belasco, 2014: 15).

11 The World Bank does not provide GDP data for Iraq between 1991 and 2003.

12 According to the World Bank, Iraq's GDP between 2004 and 2008 was respectively 36, 50, 65, 89 and 132, while the expense of US operations between 2003 and 2008 was, according to the US Department of Defence (2019: 12), 55, 75, 90, 125 and 140 billion, respectively. However, other sources estimate higher amounts (Belasco, 2014: 15).

13 The UK expected to spend more than 30 billion in Afghanistan and another 14 in Iraq, or Germany's military participation in Afghanistan which accounted for more than 15 billion until 2011 (Crawford, 2016: 19).

Bibliography

Bearak, Max and Lazaro Gamio (2016), "The U.S. Foreign Aid Budget, Visualized", *The Washington Post*, 18 October.

Belasco, Amy (2014), *The Cost of Iraq, Afghanistan, and Other Global War on Terror Operations Since 9/11*, Congressional Research Service, ref. RL33110, 8 December.

Bridey, Jean-Jacques (2018), *Rapport Fait au Nom de la Commission de la Défense Nationale et des Forces Armées sur le Projet de Loi (n° 659) relatif à la programmation militaire pour les années 2019 à 2025 et portant diverses dispositions intéressant la défense*, National Assembly, No 765, 14 March.

Chivers, C. J. (2016), "How Many Guns Did the U.S. Lose Track of in Iraq and Afghanistan? Hundreds of Thousands", *The New York Times*, 24 August.

Cour des Comptes (2016), *Les Opérations Extérieures de la France 2012–2015. Communication à la commission des finances du Sénat*, October.

Crawford, Neta C. (2016), *US Budgetary Costs of Wars through 2016: $4.79 Trillion and Counting. Summary of Costs of the US Wars in Iraq, Syria, Afghanistan and Pakistan and Homeland Security*, Watson Institute, September.

Daggett, Stephen (2010), *Costs of Major U.S. Wars*, 29 June, Congressional Research Service, ref. RS22926.

Font, Tica and Eduardo Melero (2016), *Spanish Arms Exports 2006–2015. Spanish Weapons Used in Middle East Conflicts*, Centre Delàs for Peace Studies.

Giraud, Joël (2017), *Rapport Fait au Nom de la Commission des Finances, de l'Économie Générale et du Contrôle Budgétaire sur le Projet de Loi Finances pour 2018 (n° 235). Annexe 14- Défense : Budget Opérationnel de la Défense*, National Assembly, n° 273, 12 October.

González, Miguel (2018), "Spain Beats Its Own Record with €4.3 Billion in Weapons Exports", *El País*, 15 May.

Martin, Loretta P., Teresa de Fortuny, and Xavier Bohigas (2012), *Piracy in Somalia: An Excuse or a Geopolitical Opportunity?*, Centre Delàs for Peace Studies.

Ministry of Defence of France (2019), "Carte des opérations et missions militaires", updated 5 August, https://www.defense.gouv.fr/operations/rubriques_complementaires/carte-des-operations-et-missions-militaires (Last accessed: 25 September 2019).

Ministry of Defence of Spain (2019), "Misiones Internacionales", update 1 January, http://www.defensa.gob.es/Galerias/defensadocs/misiones-internacionales.pdf (Last accessed: 25 September 2019).

NATO (2019), "Defence Expenditure of NATO Countries (2012–2019)", 25 June, https://www.nato.int/nato_static_fl2014/assets/pdf/pdf_2019_06/20190625_PR2019-069-EN.pdf (Last accessed: 22 September 2019).

OCHA (2019), "Financial Tracking Service", UN Office for the Coordination of Humanitarian Affairs, https://fts.unocha.org/ (Last accessed: 29 September 2019).

Ortega, Pere, Xavier Bohigas, and Xavier Mojal (2017), *The Absurdity of Military Spending. Analysis of the Budget of Defence in Spain, 2017*, Centre Delàs for Peace Studies, June.

Pozo Marín, Alejandro (2008), *Alliance of Barbarities. Afghanistan 2001–2008 10 Reasons to Question (and Rethink) Foreign Involvement*, Centre Delàs for Peace Studies, December.

Pozo Marín, Alejandro (2019), "Rethinking Foreign Military Operations. The Case of Spain" in Calvo Rufanges, Jordi (2019): *Security Policies for Peace. Another Security Is Possible and Necessary*, Centre Delàs for Peace Studies, 77–90, Barcelona.

Sánchez, Álvaro and Lucía Abellán (2019), "El gasto militar se estanca en España pese a las presiones de Trump", *El País*, 26 June.

Sénat of France (n.d.), "Projet de loi de finances pour 2019: Défense: Préparation et emploi des forces", http://www.senat.fr/rap/a18-149-6/a18-149-62.html (Last accessed: 27 September 2019).

SIPRI (2019), "Military Expenditure by Country, in Constant (2017) US$ m., 1988–2018", https://www.sipri.org/sites/default/files/Data%20for%20all%20countries %20from%201988%E2%80%932018%20in%20constant%20%282017%29%20 USD%20%28pdf%29.pdf (Last accessed: 28 September 2019).

Todorov, Tzvetan (2012), "Orgullosos de nuestra fuerza", *El País*, 8 July.

US Department of Defence (2018), *Cost of War through December 31, 2017*, Federation of American Scientists.

Wezeman, Pieter D., Aude Fleurant, Alexandra Kuimova, Nan Tian, and Siemon T. Wezeman (2019), *Trends in International Arms Transfers*, 2018, SIPRI Factsheet, March.

Woodward, F. Matthew (2018), *Funding for Overseas Contingency Operations and Its Impact on Defense Spending*, Congressional Budget Office, October.

4 Empire, US military spending and campaigning for a moral budget

Joseph Gerson

4.1 Introduction

As the Stockholm International Peace Research Institute's annual global military spending report demonstrates, the United States is not the world's only nation with a significant military industrial complex. Indeed, the political and economic systems of a number of lesser powers are impacted by institutions devoted to production of the machines of murder and coercion. However, with US military spending exceeding the combined total of the world's eight next greatest military spenders, the United States has become an exceedingly militarized society with a nearly uninterrupted history of war fighting. The roughly one trillion dollars that the United States spends annually for its military and related institutions is an expression of empire, albeit an empire in decline.

Because the origins of the US government lie in its anti-colonial Declaration and War of Independence, it has long been politically taboo to refer to what the United States has created as an empire. Yet, any honest reading of US history informs us that the Greek, Roman, British, Spanish and French empires were the models for the country's founding fathers. As the author of the Declaration of Independence and the United States' third president, Thomas Jefferson, put it: "I am persuaded no constitution was ever before as well calculated as ours for extensive empire and self-government" (Williams, 1980). Among the questions debated during the 1789 Constitutional Convention were how expansive the metropolitan centre should be, and how fast the empire should expand.

Over the course of the19th century, reinforced by superior fire power and a tide of millions of immigrants, Euro-Americans conquered and bought a continental empire, inflicted genocide on the Native Americans, accumulated capital and built an infrastructure on the backs of slave and exploited immigrant labour, exploited spectacular natural resources, and raised protectionist tariff walls.

Once that continental empire was consolidated, and a navy created in the 1890s that could contest Britain and other colonial powers on the high seas, US leaders moved to create what became its international empire. In the last years of the 19th century, the United States seized much of Spain's empire. Cuba and Puerto Rico were conquered thereby cementing US control of the Caribbean and most of Latin America. And the brutal conquests of the Philippines, Guam and Samoa provided the United States with the fuelling stations and bases needed to join the colonial plunder of China.

The United States was a reluctant entrant into the First World War. During the nearly four-year period of its official neutrality, the US economy became the major supplier of civilian and war materials to European combatants, making "the ultimate conversion of the economy to a wartime basis easier than it otherwise would have been" (Rockoff, 2004). Even before the 1941 Japanese attack on Pearl Harbor and US entry into the Second World War, the United States was transforming its peacetime economy to supply warplanes and other weapons to the British and French. Anticipating US entry into the war, in 1940 President Roosevelt called for the "production of 185,000 aeroplanes, 120,000 tanks, 55,000 anti-aircraft guns and 18 million tons of merchant shipping" (Katzaroff, 2017). By the war's end 300,000 planes, and two-thirds of allied military equipment had been produced in the United States.

The organization of finance, workers, technology and logistics to prevail in these wars required the creation of a military-industrial complex. Electric Boat, one of the two companies that later merged to create the world's fifth largest weapons manufacturer, was created in 1899 to build "torpedo boats." Lockheed-Martin, now the world's largest weapons company, began as the Lockheed and Martin Companies in 1912, merging in 1955 during the Cold War. And Boeing, now number two, was established in 1916 to manufacture aircraft for the coming war. Other now familiar names were also involved: Smith and Wesson, Springfield, Browning.

Among others, the wealth and power of the Bush family, known in recent decades as the authors of disastrous wars against Iraq and for their ties with the corrupt and brutal Saudi monarchy, has its roots in four generations of weapons production beginning with the manufacture of gun forgings for US troops in the First World War. (Kevin Philipps. *American Dynasty: Aristocracy, Fortune, and the Politics of Deceit in the House of Bush*, 2004.)

In the aftermath of the Great War, considerable blame for the disastrous conflagration was directed against, what President Roosevelt had termed in 1934 *the merchants of the engines of destruction*. In Congress Senator Nye skewered the arms manufacturers, and many companies, including Dupont, were called out for making massive profits with their contributions to German rearmament once Hitler came to power.

What had been the antecedents of the military-industrial complex were transformed into the world's most powerful munitions system as the United States moved towards war in 1940. In the words of Elberton Smith, the official army historian of the mobilization, the relationship "was gradually transformed from an 'arm's length' relationship between two more or less equal parties [government and business] in a business transaction into an undefined but intimate relationship" (Higgs, 1995).

US military spending expanded exponentially, as did the profits of munitions manufacturers. Between 1922 and 1939, US military budgets averaged $744 million a year. But, "between mid-1940 and late 1941 ... Congress appropriated $36 billion for the War Department alone – more than the army and navy combined had spent during World War I." Secretary of War Henry Stimson observed that, "If you are going to try to go to war, or to prepare for war, in a capitalistic country, you have got to let business make money out of the process or business won't work" (Higgs, 1995).

Even then, the military industry was highly centralized.

> The top 100 prime contractors received about two-thirds of the awards by value; the top 10 got about 30 percent...The military research and development contracts ...were even more concentrated. The top 68 corporations got two-thirds of the R&D awards; the top ten took in nearly two-fifths of the total.
>
> (Higgs, 1995)

With what Samuel P. Huntington termed the United States' superiority in applying "organized violence" the United States emerged from the wars against Germany and Japan as the world's dominant power. Known to only a few US Americans then and now, in 1948, George Kennan, the author of Washington's Cold War "containment" doctrine directed against the Soviet Union, wrote a remarkable top-secret memo while serving as head of Policy Planning at the US State Department. Among other things, he advised:

> We have about 50% of the world's wealth, but only 6 percent of its population.... In this situation, we cannot fail to be the object of envy and resentment. Our real task in the coming period is to devise a pattern of relationship which will permit us to maintain this position of disparity.... We need not deceive ourselves that we can afford today the luxury of altruism and world-benefaction.... We should cease to talk about, argue and...unreal objectives such as human rights, the raising of the living standard and democratization. The day is not far off when we are going to have to deal in straight power concepts. The less we are then hampered by idealistic slogans, the better.
>
> (Gerson, 2007)

Of course, the United States had already obliterated Hiroshima and Nagasaki with the world's first nuclear weapons in its futile effort to avoid sharing imperial influence with the Soviet Union in Manchuria, northern China and Korea.

Today, as the US National Strategy decreases its emphasis on counterterrorism to concentrate on confronting China and Russia, the US Empire is in decline. Unlike 1948, when European and Japanese industries and economies remained devastated from the war, they have taken back major shares of the global economy. China has risen and is now an economic and increasingly military peer competitor with the United States. And, like the Roman Empire, which collapsed under the weight of the corruptions of militarism and a political system overwhelmed by ill-gotten wealth (Beard, 2015), the United States has become an increasingly militarized plutocracy.

4.2 Increasing military spending

The power to create less militarist and transformed US foreign and military policies will be limited by the vested interests of the military-industrial-Congressional complex, by the many American politicians who are wedded to the military industrial complex and to the corporations and wealthy donors who fund their election campaigns. Years ago, during the Reagan Administration's shockingly rapid military buildup, Ulysses Torres, a Chilean Methodist minister who had been imprisoned and tortured by Pinochet's military dictatorship was asked, When do you know if you have a military government? His response: "Look at your national budget."[1]

Like the Italian and German fascists who were nurtured by sectors of their nations' elites, and who later came to dominate them, the US military industrial complex is a symptom and expression of the society at large, particularly its exceptionalist, white supremacist, manifest destiny empire. The military now consumes 61% of the national government's discretionary spending (National Priorities Project, 2018) and is one of the two dominant forces in the United States, the other being the plutocracy, with which it is entwined.

Donald Trump's administration and the country's militarist Congress recently increased the Pentagon's budget to $738 billion, more than 4% of GDP, bringing the Trump era military spending increases to almost $100 billion a year. That increase equals more than $72 billion euros. But there's more. The so-called intelligence community's black budget is thought to be approaching $100 billion. There is also the mis-named Department of Homeland Security, which enforces the country's increasingly militarized borders and manages the concentration camps for desperate immigrants and their separated families. Taken together, US military spending is closer to $1 trillion.

What does it pay for? Approximately $150 billion is spent to finance America's "empire of bases," more than 800 in number that extend around the world including Büchel with its nuclear weapons and Ramstein, which has been essential to fighting US wars from Afghanistan and across the Middle East and is home to AFRICOM; roughly two hundred bases and installations from South Korea to Diego Garcia that ring China, and a new generation of "lily pad" bases across Africa (Vine and Winchester, 2015).

The United States is on track to spend $1.7 trillion for a new generation of nuclear weapons and their delivery systems, reinforcing its preparations and threats to initiate nuclear war as the ultimate enforcer of empire. There are more than a million troops under arms. A naval build up is under way to reinforce US Asia–Pacific dominance. Billions are being spent for the new Space Force and offensive cyber warfare capabilities.

USA Today (2019), the largest circulation newspaper in the United States, reports that

> The government paid 30 companies at least $2.3 billion each in fiscal 2017. Four companies on this list were each awarded federal contracts worth over $14 billion – more than the entire budget for the Environmental Protection Agency or the Department of the Interior.

Last year, Lockheed–Martin, the world's largest weapons producer won $50.7 billion in contracts. Boeing, #2, got $23.4, General Dynamics $15.3 billion, Raytheon, based in my home state of Massachusetts, provides the missiles and warheads for Saudi Arabia's disastrous war on Yemen, and took in $14.7 billion (USA Today, 2019).

4.3 How the system works

How is it paid for? In 2018 the average taxpayer sent $3,456 to the Pentagon and only $39 to the Environmental Protection Agency (Johnson, 2018). But taxes haven't covered all the costs for US weapons systems, for its more than one million men and women under arms, for the tens of thousands of military contractors, and for the veterans of the country's endless wars.

Ironically, because of the symbiotic relationship between the US and Chinese economies, much of the deficit has been covered by the sale of US bonds to China. Even before future generations have to redeem those bonds, the US people are paying for Donald Trump's administration military increases with a 36% cut in environmental programmes, a 35% cut in housing and community programmes, a 41% cut in the State Department and foreign aid (Ellis, 2018) and 700,000 losing food assistance.

How does the system work? In 1960, on leaving office, President Eisenhower warned that "In the councils of government, we must guard against the acquisition of unwarranted influence, whether sought or unsought, by the military–industrial complex." He also warned that "Every gun that is made, every warship launched, every rocket fired signifies, in the final sense, a theft from those who hunger and are not fed, those who are cold and are not clothed" (Eisenhower, 1961).

The military-industrial-Congressional complex has devised an elegant system to ensure that their privileges endure. To win the votes of members of Congress, weapons manufacturers like Lockheed–Martin, Boeing, General Dynamics and Raytheon have dispersed the production of the components of massive weapons systems to hundreds of Congressional districts across the country. It is the most exceptional member of Congress who won't fight to bring these subcontracts and the related jobs back to their districts. They call it *bringing the bacon back home*. Thus, even progressive Democrats, including Bernie

Sanders who supports the F-35s being based in Vermont and Elizabeth Warren, long associated with her home state's Raytheon, vote to keep the system going.

Another military spending dynamic has gone under the radar. With cyber and high-tech warfare at the cutting edges of military development and power, and with its big bucks, the Pentagon is snatching up whatever it can. In high-tech centres like Cambridge, Massachusetts and Silicon Valley in California, universities and the weapons manufacturers organize events to attract start-ups of all varieties. The Pentagon is there, shelling out hundreds of thousands of dollars, and more, to arrange purchases and investment in these technologies. Anxious to get their hands on these technologies before the Chinese can lay their money down, the deals are made on the spot, in 24 hours or if there are delays, within 48 hours.

And, as President Clinton's Secretary of State Madeleine Albright (2019) once put it, ""What's the point of having this superb military you're always talking about if we can't use it?" Thus, former President Jimmy Carter recently taught that the United States is "the world's most warlike nation," having been at peace for only 16 years of its 242 years as a nation.

4.4 Campaigning to reduce US military spending

There is a broad range of grassroots peace, justice and social needs organizations working to cut US military spending. These initiatives are fed by a growing number of think tanks, ranging from the National Priorities Project, the Institute for Policy Studies and the Centre for International Policy on the left to the CATO institute on the libertarian right.

Led by the International Peace Bureau and community-based groups, Global Days of Action protests have been launched across the United States in recent years, with 25 events in 2019. Perhaps the most dynamic and influential was the Boston Tax Day protest. Local organizers, led by Massachusetts Peace Action, Dorchester People for Peace and the American Friends Service Committee, maximized their impact via the media by having newly elected and progressive Representative Ayana Pressley as their featured speaker. Her election platform had called for a 25% cut in US military spending in order to address her constituents' essential human needs: housing, medical care, education and the climate.

Despite the money and influence of the military-industrial complex, critics of military spending demonstrated that they represent the popular will in the more progressive states. In 2012, with no money, a coalition of peace and social needs organizations launched a state-wide referendum in Massachusetts urging Congress to take four actions: protect and fund essential human needs and services, create green jobs with infrastructure investment and pay for these policies by cutting the military budget and increasing taxes on the wealthiest 2%. They prevailed with a 3:1 ratio across the state, sending a powerful message to the state's Congressional delegation (Americans Friends Service, 2019). Many of them have since voted against the military budget.

More recently, a consortium of Washington area liberal and libertarian think tanks, concerned that the country's National Defense Strategy undermines US security, internationally and domestically, has issued an alternative strategy calling for reducing the Pentagon budget by more than $100 billion annually over the next decade. They note that the United States is "relatively safe by historical standards from conventional attack," that the last 18 years of war in "Afghanistan have done more harm than good," and that neither Russia nor China "pose a traditional threat to the United States." They note that "the most urgent risks to US security are non-military": climate change, uncontrollable migration, cyber-attacks and disease epidemics. Hardly pacifists, they are also committed to a war on wasteful Pentagon spending to make the US military more effective (Sustainable Defense Task Force, 2010).

Seeking greater structural and political change, and in the tradition of Martin Luther King, progressive think tanks associated with the Poor People's Campaign, are advocating passage of a "Moral Budget." It calls for "sav[ing] as much as $350 million per year by cutting current Pentagon spending for fighting endless wars, maintaining a worldwide network of 800 military bases, stoking dangerous arms races, and subsidizing for-profit corporate contractors." Even with those cuts, the authors of the report advise, "our military budget would still be larger than that of China, Russia, and Iran combined" (Barnes, Koshgharian and Siddique (2019).

4.5 Conclusion

In many ways, the outlook in the United States remains grim. The country's democratic values and institutions are at risk. The military is the nation's most respected institution. Conservatives and militarists are well on their way to creating an autocratic national security state. Many young people can't afford the education they deserve. Housing costs are reaching astronomical levels. Life expectancy is decreasing, and Trump and his cronies are at war with the environment.

But resistance is strong, especially from young people and people of colour who clearly understand where their interests lie. Peace, justice, environmental and democracy organizations are working to build intersectional movements based on recognition of the common sources of existential threats and oppression: militarism, the climate emergency, poverty and racism. Increasingly movements are recognizing the urgency of building cross-issue coalitions and alliances to build the people's power needed to win local and national victories.

In time, three dynamics will intersect, but how long this will take and how many lives will be lost or truncated before then remain the unknown. First is the cumulative effect of outrage and the recognition that some industries and jobs are fundamentally evil and should cease to exist. Second is pragmatism and the compassionate commitment to investing in life-affirming and environmentally sustainable economic transitions. Finally, there is the steady decline of empire.

Note

1 Author's notes (1983).

Bibliography

Albraight, Madeleine (2019), "U.S. The Most Warlike Nation." Common Dreams, February 18th.

Americans Friends Service (2019), Budget for All Massachusetts Referendum, https://www.afsc.org/resource/budget-all-massachusetts-referendum, Accessed on 21 December 2019

Bacevich, Andrew J. (2010), *Washington Rules: America's Path to Permanent War*, New York: Metropolitan Books.

Barnes, Koshgharian and Siddique (2019), *Poor People's Moral Budget: Everybody Has the Right to Live*, Institute for Policy Studies.

Barnet, Richard J. (1982), *The Alliance: America-Europe: Japan Makers of the Postwar World*, New York: Simon & Schuster.

Beard, Mary (2015), *SPQR A History of Ancient Rome*, London: Profile Books.

Brzezinski, Zbigniew (1997), *The Grand Chessboard: American Primacy and Its Geostrategic Imperatives*, New York: Basic Books.

Cumings, Bruce (2009), *Dominion from Sea to Sea: Pacific Ascendancy and American Power*, New Haven: Yale University Press.

Derber, Charles (2017), *Welcome to the Revolution: Universalizing Resistance*, New York: Routledge.

Eisenhower, Dwight (1961): *Farewell address delivered 17 January 1961, available at American Rethoric:* https://americanrhetoric.com/speeches/dwightdeisenhowerfarewell.html, accessed 18 January 2020

Ellis, Niv (2018), "Spending Deal Cuts $3.4 Billion from State and Foreign Operations", The Hill, March 21st 2018.

Gerson, Joseph (2007), *Empire and the Bomb: How the U.S. Uses Nuclear Weapons to Dominate the World*. London: Pluto Press.

Gerson, Joseph and Bruce Birchard, eds. (1991), *The Sun Never Sets... Confronting the Network of Foreign U.S. Military Bases*, Boston: South End Press.

Higgs, Robert (1995), "World War II and the Military-Industrial-Congressional Complex, Independent Institute, https://www.independent.org/publications/article.asp?id=141, Accessed on 18 December 2019

Huntington, Samuel P. (1996), *The Clash of Civilizations and the Remaking of World Order*, New York: Simon & Schuster.

Immerwahr, Daniel (2019), *How to Hide an Empire: A History of the Greater United States*, New York: Farrar, Straus and Giroux.

Johnson, Jake (2018), "Astronomical Cost of War: Average US Taxpayer Sent $3,456 to Pentagon". Common Dreams.

Katzaroff, Paul (2017), *The Reluctant Traveler: Memoirs of World War Two*, Bloomington: Aurthorhouse.

McCoy, Alfred W. (2007), *In the Shadows of the American Century*, Chicago: Haymarket Books.

National Priorities Project (2018), "Trump's FY2019 Budget Request Has Massive Cuts for Nearly Everything But the Military", National Priorities Project.

Phililips, Kevin (2004), Am*erican Dynasty: Aristocracy, Fortune, and the Politics of Deceit in the House of Bush*, New York: Viking Penguin.

Rockoff, Hugh (2004), Until it's Over, Over There: The U.S. Economy in World War I, NBER Working Paper No. 10580.

Sustainable Defense Task Force (2010), *Debt, Deficits & Defense A Way Forward*, Sustainable Defense Task Force.

USA Today (2019), "Lockheed Martin, Boeing Get the Most Money," *USA Today*, March 27th 2019.

Vine, David and Winchester, Simon (2017), *Base Nation: How U.S. Military Bases Harm the United States and the World*, New York: Metropolitan Books.

Williams, William Appleman (1980), *Empire as a Way of Life*, New York: Oxford University Press.

Williams, William Appleman, ed. (1972), *From Colony to Empire: Essays in the History of American Foreign Relations*, New York: John Wily and Sons.

Williams, William Appleman (1959), *The Tragedy of American Diplomacy*, New York: Delta Books.

5 Militarisation of the European Union

Fresh money for the military industry

Laëtitia Sédou, Mark Akkerman and Bram Vranken

5.1 Introduction

Angela Merkel and Emmanuel Macron mentioned in November 2018 the idea of creating a real European army (Gros-Verheyde, 2018). Federica Mogherini, the EU High Representative for Foreign Affairs and Security, and Jean-Claude Juncker, the EU Commission President, have been regularly priding themselves on having done more for a European Union of Defence in the past few years than their predecessors in decades.

The objective of this analysis isn't to conduct an exhaustive academic analysis about European Defence or about the concept of militarisation. That can be found in Karampekios, Oikonomou et al. (2018) or Bartels, Kellner et al. (2017), among others. Our aim is to shed light on precise outcomes having a decisive impact on military spending and on the EU project cornerstones. In order to do it we will focus on recent developments that are (1) taking place within the EU competences (that is laws or policies jointly adopted by the EU Member States and the European Parliament, and whose implementation is the responsibility of the European Commission), and (2) affecting the EU budget (the policy or programme is funded by the EU 'common pot').

Therefore, we won't address purely intergovernmental developments (that is decisions made collectively by the EU Member States only, mostly funded through extra national contributions and on which the European Parliament and Commission play hardly no role). Military-related issues had been so far dealt with that way, under the CFSP (Common Foreign and Security Policy) or the CSDP (Common Security and Defence Policy) framework: for example, military or civilian joint missions abroad, the European Defence Agency (EDA, an intergovernmental structure to strength defence capabilities at EU, or PESCO (the Permanent Structured Cooperation, a framework for projects). We will only briefly refer to these initiatives when they are directly related to our topic.

Not that those developments are not important per se, but they are of a different nature and have been running and evolving slowly but surely for more than a decade now (the EDA was created in 2004, and PESCO was launched in December 2017) in particular on the basis of the Lisbon Treaty of 2009.

In turn, the recent initiatives we want to address in this paper, foreshadow a more fundamental paradigm shift of the EU project, directly affect the EU budget, and their legitimacy and legality are still contested (Fischer-Lescano, 2018).

Moreover it will be explored how the EU Defence Action Plan (European Commission, 2016), presented in November 2016 by Jean-Claude Juncker, and all the initiatives resulting from it, might reflect at least some of those indicators of EU militarisation and increased military spending; in particular direct funding to the military sector like the European Defence Fund but also the mobilisation of other – civilian – programmes for military purposes, Then it will be pointed out how EU responses to policing and security challenges are evolving and might amount to militarisation too. Indeed, securitisation is often an important step on the way towards militarisation. According to Buzan, Wæver et al. (1998) an issue is securitised when it is considered an existential threat, requiring urgent action, justifying measures outside the normal political process. Many large societal problems, for example, climate change and its consequences or forced migration, are increasingly framed as security threats. The military and security industry plays a big part in this framing, positioning themselves as experts and offering the solution: the use of its goods and services.

Finally, the role of the industry will be a topic to develop before drawing conclusions, delving into the importance of arms industry lobbying to make those developments happen, and reflecting the emergence of a European military-industrial complex over-influencing EU policy-making.

5.2 Using the EU budget to answer perceived military needs

On 30 November 2016, the President of the European Commission (EC) Jean-Claude Juncker presented its European Defence Action Plan (EDAP) to the European Parliament. This document listed a number of initiatives in the military domain that the European Union should undertake, in particular "«launching a European Defence Fund", "fostering investments in defence supply chains" and "reinforcing the single market for defence" (European Commission, 2016: 5).

5.2.1 The first steps

But such Plan did not come out of the blue, and previous steps were already taken as pilot initiatives. In 2007, a European Security Research Programme was integrated into the EU Research Framework Programme (FP7), and was then extended in 2014 with an increased budget, in order to Fund industrial research in the security and dual-use areas. An Internal Security Fund was also created in 2014 to finance member states' strengthening of their security infrastructures.

The 2013 EC Communication 'Towards a more competitive and efficient defence and security sector' started analysing the shortages of the European military industry and proposed a number of actions the EU could take, as a way to contribute to perceived military capabilities needs and to the EU's strategic autonomy.

Actions ranged from deepening the internal market for military goods, strengthening industrial competitiveness in particular for small and medium enterprises (SMEs), exploiting as much as possible civilian-military synergies, as well as exploring «new avenues (…) and preparing the ground for more and deeper European cooperation» in particular via «the possibility of EU-owned dual-use capabilities» and considering «launching a preparatory action for CSDP-related research» (European Commission, 2013: 4–5).

In 2014, the EU Council and Parliament agreed to start a Pilot project on CSDP-related research,[1] with an envelope of €1.5 million taken from the EU budgets of 2015 and 2016.

In February 2015, the EU Commissioner for Industry, Elżbieta Bieńkowska, set up a High Level 'Group of Personalities on Defence Research' (GoP), dominated by profit-making groups (see Chapter IV). The GoP final report was published in February 2016, and in the following months most of its recommendations were taken over by the EU: as a start, a Preparatory Action for Defence Research (PADR)[2] was integrated in the 2017 budget, with a total budget of €90 million over 2017–2019.

5.2.2 The European Defence Fund: new subsidies for military Research & Development

EU Pilot projects and Preparatory Actions are meant to be testing schemes and, according to results produced, may pave the way for a proper EU funding programme. However, in this particular case, the agenda accelerated in an unexpected manner in 2017. On 7 June, the day when the PADR first calls for proposals were just published, the European Commission also presented two new legislative proposals marking a jump in size and scope:

- One proposal was to create a European Defence Industrial Development Programme – the EDIDP (European Commission, 2017a) to start in January 2019, which would dedicate €500 million to the second phase of a Research & Development (R&D) process (the research phase being covered by the Preparatory Action); the Council and Parliament agreed on the EDIDP Regulation in less than a year, in May 2018.
- The second paper was a Communication launching the European Defence Fund for 2021–2027 (European Commission, 2017b), which was followed by a legislative proposal in May 2018 (European Commission, 2018a); the Fund will support both research and development projects with a proposed total budget of €13 billion (€4.1bn for research and €8.9bn for development). The final adoption of this Fund is expected

by the end of 2019, and derogatory rules bar the European Parliament from effective oversight and influence over its implementation during its entire duration.

It is also important to stress that this EU funding is an add-on to national military spending, not a substitute: the European Commission regularly insists that EU Member States should in parallel continue increasing their military budgets in order to meet NATO targets.

a) *A Fund to boost arms industry competitiveness and answer military capabilities needs for operational capacity*

There are two main arguments to justify creating a European Defence Fund.

First the needs of the European Defence Technological and Industrial Base (EDTIB): according to the EC's analysis as developed in all key documents since 2013, the European military industry suffers from inefficiency in spending due to duplications, a lack of interoperability and technological gaps. The Commission claims that EU countries would better answer those challenges by pooling resources together, as the current pace of innovation makes it impossible for most, if not all, EU countries to develop and maintain alone the critical technologies and capabilities required for the future.

This leads us to the second argument, i.e. EU member states needs in terms of military capabilities: according to the promoters of the Defence Fund, reinforcing the EDTIB is a necessity in order to answer the military needs of EU Members States in terms of capabilities, so that their armed forces have at their disposal sufficient and efficient military equipment and weaponry to face challenges and threats, and to guarantee EU's strategic autonomy and operational capacity.

b) *A Fund for the development of the next generation of weaponry contributing to a global arms race*

Funding will go to applied research centres from the security sector and weapons manufacturers, but also to civilian companies working on technologies relevant for the military like artificial intelligence. Those companies are indeed an explicit target, and one aim of the funding is to convince them to enter the military supply chain via generous granting conditions.

Another example of how EU initiatives like the Defence Fund and PESCO are triggering a new emphasis on military priorities and funding is Flanders: for almost 25 years, the Flemish government had as a policy not to invest public money in military research and development. However in July 2018 the Minister for Innovation Philippe Muyters announced that VLAIO, the regional agency for industrial R&D policy (previously called IWT), would start public investments in military R&D; this change was made in order to facilitate access of its industry to the Defence Fund (which requests Member

States' co-funding for some types of development projects). And in countries like Ireland, military-related EU developments raise harsh debates about a possible threat to their neutrality.

The Fund will be open to companies based and controlled in the EU or other European countries (Norway, Iceland and probably the UK), and also possibly from non-European countries (like the US or Israel who already regularly partner with EU companies) under certain conditions still under negotiation.

The Fund will focus on 'cutting-edge' technologies like autonomous and unmanned systems (for example, armed drones), and intelligence-surveillance, cybersecurity and maritime security. If support for the development for 'killer-robots' will be excluded from 2021, other types of fully autonomous systems will be allowed, for «defence purposes» for example.[3] Moreover, part of the funding will be earmarked for 'disruptive technologies' which can «radically change the concept and conduct of defence affairs» (European Commission, 2018a: 22).

By doing so, EU subsidies are meant to «boost the global competitiveness» of the European arms industry, and one of their expected results is to increase exports outside the EU (European Commission, 2013: 15, 2017a: 19). This will contribute to the global race between traditional and emerging military powers for developing the next generation of weaponry, and for market shares worldwide.

To sum-up, the European Union is due to spend €13.59 billion over a decade (2017–2027) to answer what are perceived as military needs at both industrial and strategic levels, if the Defence Fund for 2021–2027 is adopted as proposed. These industrial subsidies will be an add-on to national military spending, and Member States' contributions as co-funding for development projects could amount to up to €37.6 billion.

5.2.3 Alleged military-industrial needs to be mainstreamed across all European programmes

The EU will also use other avenues to support the military-industrial complex. The EC decided to facilitate the access of arms companies to a range of EU funding opportunities, what the EC calls 'fostering investments in defence supply chains', as a way to support the competitiveness of this sector. It proposed first an increased use of the EU Structural Funds (ESIF) in particular the Regional Development Fund in order to encourage the creation of 'regional clusters of excellence' in the field of defence,[4] and also the European Social Fund and the Cohesion Fund. It also opened access to COSME funds (Programme for the Competitiveness of Enterprises and SMEs), and the arms sector became a priority under the new Skills Agenda for Europe, by supporting an «industry-led European Defence Skills Alliance» and making use of funds like Erasmus+, the EU programme for education, training, youth and sport.

The Action Plan also included a call to the Member States to adopt the lending criteria of the European Investment Bank (EIB), which are so far excluding investments in projects related to weapons production and sale. This move would in particular open access to the €21 billion guarantee Fund of the European Fund for Strategic Investment (EFSI, also called the Juncker Plan) for the arms industry. For the time being this proposal has been blocked by the European Parliament and the EIB President Werner Hoyer.

However the bank can already invest in security or dual-use projects provided they focus on civilian applications only, and will dedicate €6 billion over three years through a 'European Security Initiative' (adopted early 2018) to support RDI (Research, Development and Innovation) for dual-use technologies, cybersecurity and civilian security infrastructure. EIB Vice-President Alexander Stubb also signed a Memorandum of Understanding with the EU Defence Agency (EDA) in February 2018.

As a result, there is a clear trend towards considering the production and sale of weapons and military technology as a 'normal' business and a priority, in order to support the military industry across Europe. Because this support is included in larger programmes, it is extremely difficult to figure out how much money will be made available to the military sector.[5]

5.3 Adapting resources or technology such as transport infrastructure, skills or space for military use

We have seen to which extent the recent EU initiatives are meant to answer perceived military needs via financial support to the military industry. Other initiatives go beyond that and also aim at adapting resources or technology for a military use, another dimension of a militarisation process, while also contributing to military spending growth. Without claiming to be exhaustive, some recent examples are illustrative.

The 2016 Defence Action Plan already stated that «Furthermore, the Commission will promote civil/military synergies within EU policies, wherever appropriate» (European Commission, 2016: 5). And the EC President Juncker made even clearer in his 'State of the Union' address in 2017 that 'defence' is now one of the main objectives of the EU, aiming at a 'Defence Union'[6] by 2025 (Juncker, 2017).

As a consequence, all Commissioners have been asked to look for ways to answer military needs in their own field of action: «For each portfolio we had to think about what we could do in our field» said Transport Commissioner Violeta Bulc in November 2017 when presenting its Military Mobility Action Plan (European Commission, 2018b). Announced in the Defence Action Plan, this Plan was adopted by the Commission in March 2018. As described by Transport Commissioner Violeta Bulc,

> The aim of the Action Plan is to improve the mobility of military forces within and beyond the EU, allowing the EU and its Member States to

act faster, in line with their defence needs and responsibilities – both in the context of Common Security and Defence Policy missions and operations, as well as national and multinational activities (e.g. in the framework of NATO).

(Bulc, 2018)

Actions will be taken in two main areas, after the identification and Member States' agreement on the military requirements was carried out in 2018:

First, transport infrastructure should be assessed to identify obstacles to military mobility, such as the height clearance or weight tolerance of bridges, the loading capacity of transport by rail, or multimodal platforms for the quick shift of assets from ports and airports to rail and road. The Connecting Europe Facility (the EU programme for trans-European infrastructures) will then Fund projects for the upgrade of infrastructures covering military requirements: €6.5 billion are earmarked for this in the next EU budgetary cycle for 2021–2027.

The second area of action relates to regulatory and procedural issues: the objective is to ease the transport of dangerous military goods, to simplify customs formalities for military operations, and to facilitate permissions for cross-border movement of troops, for both surface (road, rail and inland waterways) and air movements. The EDA, the Member States and the European Commission will have to identify obstacles or gaps, and consider whether to adapt existing common rules of the civilian sector or set up new harmonised provisions that would better suit military activities.

Defence was also selected as one of six pilot sectors of the new Skills Agenda for Europe (European Commission, 2017c), an initiative to respond to skills mismatches in specific industrial sectors. The rationale is that:

> The European Defence Fund (EDF) is addressing Europe's future security needs by introducing means to support the complete capability development cycle: from research, through development, to acquisition. A successful EDF relies on technological skills being available to the industry to develop and produce common capabilities. A successful fund relies on industry's access to technological skills to create common capabilities. EU countries funding joint development projects will face increasing pressure on their pool of skills, calling for action. Europe needs the security of supply and strategic autonomy. This means ensuring defence-specific skills in several technologically advanced areas for effective and efficient production, and ultimately acquisition of capabilities.

(European Commission, 2020)

The objective is to answer the skills shortage the arms industry is facing. And this translates into very concrete actions. According to the same webpage, a «first COSME-funded project kicked-off in March 2018. An industry-led

European Defence Skills Partnership was set up». This partnership gathers 30 entities from nine EU countries: industry, academia, public authorities, research and vocational organisations. And the European Defence Skills Partnership (EDSP) was recently selected for a €4 million project under Erasmus +.[7] In this partnership appear major arms companies like Airbus, Safran, SAAB, Leonardo and Rolls-Royce.

The same can be seen in areas related to the next generation of weaponry, like artificial intelligence, digital technology and space. As seen in Chapter I, artificial intelligence and new technologies are part of the priorities under the Defence Fund, in order to adapt civilian applications for military use. Moreover, several major actors in space are also active in the military domain like Airbus, Leonardo and Thales, and as such already benefit from EU programmes for civilian and dual-use projects, and probably soon also for military-related activities under the current trend previously described.

However, beyond specific programmes and funding, structural changes illustrate a more fundamental shift: the creation of a Directorate-General for Defence Industry and Space in the new Commission to be headed by Ursula von der Leyen, former Defence Minister in Germany. It will be one of the three DGs under the responsibility of the Commissioner for Internal Market, which will be the French national Thierry Breton, former CEO of Atos.

Also illustrative is the fact that Defence and Space will be grouped under a single Directorate and that both areas are now almost systematically referred to jointly both in speeches and in writing. And the Mission letter to Thierry Breton is crystal clear: he will lead the work on a coordinated European approach on artificial intelligence and the new Digital Services Act, as well as on all military-related issues (EU Defence Fund, European Defence equipment market, military mobility…). But he is also expressly tasked to «improve the crucial link between space and defence and security [as well as] support the Member States in increasing the uptake of Galileo Public Regulated Service, which can be used [...] for emergency services, peacekeeping operations and crisis management» (von der Leyen, 2019).

Lastly, in the proposed EU Budgetary cycle for 2021–2027, €16 billion are earmarked for the Space policy. If nothing suggests that these €16 billion will be exclusively used for military-related projects, the blurring of the line between what is civilian and military (named 'synergies' by the Commission), the over-emphasis put on an 'EU that protects' and on EU Defence as a priority, combined with the over-influence of the arms industry lobbying, it can be concluded that a significant part of it will serve military purposes. «Space is also becoming an area where the EU wants to develop technology jointly, particularly as China, Russia and the United States develop space weapons that can shut down enemy missiles and air defences or destroy satellites» (Emmott, 2019).

5.4 From securitisation to militarisation of external borders and foreign policy

5.4.1 Escalating spending on border militarisation[8]

Especially since the start of the 'refugee crisis' in 2015 the EU and its member states have rapidly boosted and militarised border security. The underlying narrative, that migration is primarily a security threat to Europe, has been successfully pushed by the military and security industry. This industry is also the main beneficiary from the escalating spending on border militarisation. Furthermore, many of the leading companies, including Airbus, Leonardo and Thales, have also been major arms exporters to the Middle East and Africa, fuelling the reasons people are forced to flee.

EU Member States have been sending armed forces to the borders, erecting walls and fences and deploying an increasing amount of border security equipment, from traditional military goods (vessels, helicopters, arms) to new technologies, drones, surveillance tools and biometric identification systems. At EU-level, important steps in this process are the expansion of the border guard agency Frontex, the start of the first military operation to counter migration (Operation Sophia for the coast of Libya), increasing support from NATO, an enormous growth in funding for border security and (enforced) collaboration with third countries.

a) Frontex

In 2004 the EU established its border guard agency Frontex, whose main task is the coordination of border security efforts of the EU Member States. It also runs its own joint operations, most of them in the Mediterranean, to stop migration. Until now these operations have relied on personnel and equipment provided by Member States, who often don't live up to their promises.

In recent years Frontex has been expanded into a European Border and Coast Guard, with new tasks and competences. It will get a standing corps of 10,000 border guards, ready to be employed in 'crisis' situations, and will be able to buy equipment on its own or in co-ownership with a member state. Frontex now has a stronger supervisory role in assessing the border security capacities of Member States, including giving binding advice to take measures to strengthen these and the possibility of direct interventions in a member state, even without its consent, by decision of the Commission after consulting a committee of Member States' representatives. And it will also be able to cooperate with third countries, including the possibility of armed Frontex operations on the territory of these countries (Council of the EU, 2019).

In 2027 Frontex is expected to have an annual budget of €1.89 billion euros, over 300 times as much as the six million it started with in 2005. For

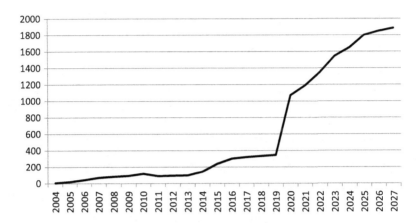

Figure 5.1 Budget Frontex (2005–2027) in €million (2020–2027: proposals).
Notes: *Of which for equipment costs: 2021, 70 €million; 2022, 175 €million; 2023, 280 €million; 2024, 330 €million; 2025, 425 €million; 2026, 445 €million; 2027, 475 €million.
Source: own elaboration.

the next EU budget cycle (2021–2027) €2.2 billion of the Frontex budget will be reserved for equipment costs. Frontex is still discussing its strategy regarding its technical equipment. This seems to come down to: lease when possible, buy when necessary. Leasing is preferred because it leaves «the through–life management responsibilities with the supplier». However, for complex systems and bespoke equipment Frontex sees ownership as the only possibility. That could also be the case when leasing leads to «unwanted non-EU supply chain dependencies», signalling a preference for buying or leasing from European industry (Frontex, 2019).

b) Funding member states' efforts

The EU heavily funds the build-up of border security by Member States. This has largely gone through three funding mechanisms: the Schengen Facility, the External Borders Fund and the Internal Security Fund – Borders. The Schengen Facility was a temporary instrument to Fund border security measures in new EU Member States, to make them comply with Schengen requirements. The External Borders Fund ran from 2007 to 2013 and was aimed at working towards a common integrated border management system. A lot of it was used for national components of the EUROSUR system.[9] And now most funding is done via the Internal Security Fund – Borders, with an emphasis on achieving a uniform control of the external EU borders and information sharing between Member States and Frontex.

Through these three funding mechanisms some €4.5 billion have been and will be allocated to EU countries, from 2004 up to next year. Funding has gone to a wide array of activities and purchases, including vessels, vehicles, helicopters, IT systems and surveillance equipment. In the next EU budget cycle to run from 2021 to 2027, the new Integrated Border Management Fund will take over from the Internal Security Fund. In the spring of 2019 the European Parliament and the Council approved the establishment of this fund, with a budget of €8 billion (Council of the EU, 2019).

c) Biometric identification systems

EU border security system encompasses more than the visual equipment at the borders. It also includes, for example, the increasing use of satellite observations, often in cooperation with the European Space Agency, and biometric identification systems. These systems, including EURODAC[10] and the Schengen Information System II (SIS II), aim to register all persons entering or trying to enter the Schengen Area, including their biometric data, and combine this information into common databases, which are accessible by all Member States to check against. EU spending on these systems has rapidly escalated since 2017. Total spending on them in the years 2000 to 2019 runs up to about €1 billion.

For Eurosur, the European Commission estimated the costs for the period 2011–2020 at 338 million euros (European Commission, 2011). The spending by Member States on Eurosur from 2013 to 2017 was estimated at around 75 million euros (European Commission, 2018c). The development of Eurosur is also supported by R&T (R & D?) financed by the EU under the so called Framework Programmes. Under the current programme, Horizon2020 (2014–2020) and its predecessor, Framework Programme 7 (2007–2013), the EU has funded research projects in the field of border security with millions of euros, including many which were (partly) aimed at developing and improving Eurosur (Hayes, 2009; Jones, 2017).

d) Cooperation with third countries

While disagreements about migration policies within the EU are getting stronger, for example, about the 'distribution' of refugees between Member States, and consensus about strengthening the security at the external borders is sometimes undermined by Member States' reluctance to provide money, personnel and equipment, there is a strong agreement about cooperation with non-EU-countries to stop refugees earlier on their way towards Europe, termed 'border externalisation'. In order to do it the EU forces third countries, notably in Africa, to act as outpost border guards through a carrot-and-stick approach. If they cooperate, they can get trade benefits, for example; if they don't cooperate, development aid, for example, is cut back

There has been a growth in border externalisation measures and agreements since 2005 and a massive acceleration since the November 2015 Valletta Europe – Africa Summit. The European Union and individual Member States are now providing a large amount of resources. This includes collaboration with third countries in terms of accepting deported persons, training of their police and border officials, the development of extensive biometric systems, and donations of equipment including helicopters, patrol ships and vehicles, surveillance and monitoring equipment. While many projects are done through the European Commission, a number of individual Member States, such as Spain, Italy and Germany also take a lead in funding and supporting border externalisation efforts through bilateral agreements with non-EU-countries. As a result there have been EU agreements with, and funding provided to, countries known for severe human rights violations, such as Chad, Niger, Belarus, Libya and Sudan.

d) Consequences

The consequences of these militarised European migration policies are highly problematic. In the first place for refugees confronted with more and more violence at the militarised borders, who are thus forced to use more dangerous migration routes when others are closed off and are driven into the hands of criminal smuggling networks. The consequences reach further though, especially when it comes to the externalisation part of these policies: from strengthening authoritarian regimes and repression to undermining political and economic stability in the countries concerned, as well as diverting and abusing development cooperation money. It is highly probable that in the long-term these policies will only lead to more refugees, thereby even undermining the EU's stated interest of 'getting the numbers down'.

5.4.2 Security for development

The shift of spending from development cooperation to border externalisation is not an isolated phenomenon. Gradually, the EU has started to militarise its foreign policy, including funding the build-up of security infrastructures in third countries, and spending more money on this. The EU seems to follow the agenda that has been pushed mostly by the German government, as summarised by Chancellor Angela Merkel: «[O]nly where security is ensured can development take place» (Deutsche Welle, 2017).

There are instruments which focus on financing activities outside Europe that also provide possibilities for military and security spending. This mainly concerns the financing of European military missions and the building and strengthening of military and security capabilities of armed forces and security forces in third countries. A start has been made on this in recent years, for example, through the expansion of the 'Instrument contributing to Stability and Peace' (IcSP). The original intention of this fund, launched in 2014, was to support conflict prevention and peace-building projects in non-EU countries. At the end of 2017, however, the European Commission decided to expand the scope of the IcSP and to make more money available. Since then, European support within the Fund can also be used for security and military actors in third countries under the Capacity Building for Security and Development (CBSD) programme with a budget of €100 million for three years. In addition, the delivery of military goods, with the exception of weapons, ammunition and lethal goods, has become possible (European Parliament, 2019). This change was preceded by a lobbying effort by the arms industry. In June 2016, the Aerospace and Defense Industries Association of Europe (ASD) already presented a proposal for expansion of the IcSP, which was largely followed in the change that was finally implemented (ASD, 2016).

For the next EU budgetary cycle (2021–2027) the Commission proposes that the IcSP and other foreign policy instruments, including human rights and development funds, are placed under an umbrella known as the 'Instrument for Neighbourhood, Development and International Cooperation' (NDICI) with a total budget of €89.5 billion. The EC proposal raises serious concerns among civil society actors as it puts a stronger emphasis on migration and security; in particular, the capacity building of military actors (CBSD) would be very prominent in the NDICI, with no ceiling as regards the amounts dedicated to it (CONCORD-EPLO-HRDN-VOICE, 2018). To add-on, a 'European Peace Facility', with an intended budget of €10.5 billion (2021–2027), will contribute to the financing of European military operations and military build-up in developing countries. This Facility is to be funded by direct national contributions, as officially EU money cannot be used for operational military expenditures.

5.5 The European military-industrial complex shaping EU policies

In 1961 President Eisenhower issued a stark and remarkable warning during his farewell address. He cautioned against the «acquisition of unwarranted influence, whether sought or unsought, by the military-industrial complex. The potential for the disastrous rise of misplaced power exists and will persist» (Eisenhower, 1961). Almost 60 years after Eisenhower's warning this military-industrial complex seems as adequate as ever, also in the European Union.

5.5.1 *A spider's web of trust and influence*

The structure of the European arms industry has changed considerably since the end of the Cold War. Although not a straightforward process, there has been a trend characterised by increasing Europeanisation and concentration of the arms industry through mergers, acquisitions and joint ventures (Oikonomou, 2008). This dynamic has led to big European arms giants such as Airbus and MBDA, a joint venture of Airbus, BAE Systems and Leonardo.

In parallel the EU became a foreign policy actor following the adoption of the Common Foreign and Security Policy pillar in 1992 with the Maastricht Treaty. These developments led to a very intimate and even symbiotic relationship between EU institutions and the arms industry, which have gone much further than what would be expected of a normal dialogue with stakeholders. Already in 2005, researcher Frank Slijper observed that

> the influence from the industry on policy-making processes is astonishing for the uninitiated outsider to see. The field of defence and defence industry would seem to have been abandoned by all but the captains of industry, the officers of the lobbies and the trusty auxiliary corps of 'sherpas'.
>
> (Slijper, 2005)

The close relationship between the European Union and the defence industry has been adequately described as «a spider's web of trust and influence» (CEO, 2011). The military-industrial complex has both the means and the access to high level decision-makers to push its interests to the top of the EU policy agenda.

5.5.2 A substantial budget with easy access to decision-makers

The European arms lobby is well represented in the EU bubble and has considerable means to push its agenda. Almost all top tier defence companies have a lobbying office in Brussels with a substantial budget. The industry's EU lobby spending was estimated in €54.7 million for 2016, based on the EU Transparency Register (Politico, 2017). The top ten European arms companies have a combined budget of approximately five million euros annually (see Figure 5.1). This is in all likelihood an underestimation as many companies under-report their lobbying budgets to the EU Transparency Register.

The influence the arms industry exerts over the EU is substantial. During the Juncker Commission the top ten arms companies and the two most important arms lobbying organisations, the European Organisation for Security (EOS) and the Aerospace and Defence Industries Association of Europe (ASD), had a total of 327 meetings with Commissioners and cabinet members. In terms of meetings, the air- and defence company Airbus is the third biggest lobbyist of the European Union with a total of 142 meetings. At the same time the ten biggest European arms companies and the lobbying organisations ASD and EOS have a total of 48 accredited lobbyists making it possible for them to freely walk in and out of the European Parliament at any time.

Arms fairs and lobbying conferences are other standard meeting places of the arms industry. Big defence and air shows not only function as a big market place of weapons, but are also a key node of industry lobbying. Conferences also function as a meeting place between the arms industry and policy

Table 5.1 Lobby of arms companies in EU

Company	Lobby expenditure	Accredited lobbyists	Meetings with Juncker Commission
BAE systems	50,000€–99,999€	1	3
Airbus	1,500,000€–1,749,000€	7	157
Thales Group	300,000€	3	23
Leonardo	300,000€–399,999€	3	35
Rolls-Royce	1,500,000€–1,749,000€	2	21
Naval group	100,000€–199,999€	3	11
Rheinmetall	300,000€–399,999€	4	1
MBDA	50,000€–99,999€	1	7
Safran	495,000€	5	11
Saab	200,000€–299,999€	5	11
ASD	298,000€	11	31
EOS	100,000€–199,999e	3	16
Total	4,893,000€–5,984,999€	49	327

Source: own elaboration based on Lobbyfacts (2019)

makers. One of the most prominent examples is the EDA annual conference. In 2018 hundreds of arms industry representatives were invited, Airbus alone received 22 invitations, meanwhile representatives of civil society were not welcome (Teffer, 2018).

The European Parliament is also host to arms industry lobbying. The Kangaroo Group is an MEP-industry forum of 'informal gatherings' for MEPs and the (defence) industry. MEPs like Michael Gahler (EPP), who has played an important role in furthering a military agenda in the Parliament, are board members of the Kangaroo Group. Another example is the Sky and Space Intergroup in the European Parliament, whose secretariat is run by the ASD. ASD boss Jan Pie has described the intergroup as «an extremely effective forum to engage with MEPs» (Vranken, 2017).

Moreover the 'spiders web' is also sustained through a rapidly spinning revolving door, where EU decision-makers end up as lobbyists and the other way around. One noteworthy case is the former defence expert for the Commission, Burkard Schmitt. Before joining the arms industry's most influential lobby group ASD in 2015, he had previously worked for more than eight years at the Commission, where, according to an internal Commission memo, he was «the pen on all matters related to defence and security» (De Correspondent, 2017).

The selection of the European Commissioner for the DG Defence Industry and Space Thierry Breton is another noteworthy case. Breton was Atos' CEO for almost ten years, a major French company with vested interests in cybersecurity, telecommunications, aerospace and defence electronics. These interests overlap significantly with the areas of work of his portfolio, including the newly created DG Defence Industry and Space. According to the lobbying watchdog Corporate Europe Observatory it might be the first time a CEO joins the College of Commissioners and his designation as Commissioner created a «maze of potential conflicts of interest» (CEO, 2019).

5.5.3 Two decades of arms lobbying

Many of the policies now being implemented by the European Union have been introduced by the arms industry during the last two decades. Already in 2002, the European Convention on the Future of Europe, the precursor of the Lisbon Treaty, established a Working Group on Defence. The Group consisted of 13 members, two of which were from arms companies (BAE Systems and EADS – the European Aeronautic Defence and Space Company – now called Airbus) and one from an arms industry lobby association, the European Defence Industries Group, EDIG, which later became the ASD (Convention for European Economic Cooperation, 2013). The president of EDIG launched the idea of exempting long-term defence investments from the Stability Pact – a proposal later included in the 2016 Defence Action Plan drafted by the European Commission.[11]

One of the most concrete outcomes of the Working Group on Defence was the establishment of the European Defence Agency (EDA) in 2004. One of the core objectives of the EDA was to promote the European defence sector's technological and industrial base. Michel Troubetzkoy, the then-head of EADS Brussels office, and director of the arms lobby group *Club Europe et Défense*, bragged at the European Agenda Summit in 2008 that the EDA was EADS' baby, and that the agency was 95% similar to EADS' proposals. Troubetzkoy also said that EADS had very easy access to Michel Barnier, who was then President of the Convention on the Future of Europe (CEO, 2008).

In 2003 the arms industry made another breakthrough. In the context of the 'War against Terror' and the take-off of a US homeland security industry, the European arms industry started pushing for a security research programme, in order not to miss out on emerging market opportunities (Hayes, 2009). In 2003 the Group of Personalities on Security Research, a Commission advisory group, played an important role in pushing this on the EU agenda. The GoP on Security Research was heavily dominated by the security and defence industry. Out of 25 members, eight members were from the arms industry (Slijper, 2005). Although military research was explicitly excluded from EU funding, the security research programme created a backdoor for the defence industry to get increasingly involved in EU research programmes.

Calls for EU military research however continued unabated. During a European Defence Agency conference in 2007, Ake Svensson, from the ASD, called on the EU to create a «Group of Wise Men to propose the agenda and conceptualize the framework in which Europe will be able to define and provide funding for important Key Technologies and Competencies» (European Defence Agency, 2007).

While this push for a fully military programme was initially opposed by Member States, the European Parliament and parts of the European Commission, consistent pressure by the military industry proved to be successful. In 2015, Industry Commissioner Bieńkowska was able to set up the Group of Personalities on Defence Research to advise her on an EU military research programme (James, 2018). The GoP was intended to provide strategic input on the European security and defence policy, but it also provided detailed advice with respect to the form, content and budget of the European Defence Fund.

The composition of the Group of Personalities was remarkable. Of its 16 members, seven represented the weapons industry (Airbus Group, BAE Systems, Finmeccanica, MBDA, Saab, Indra and the defence lobbying group ASD). Two other members represented private research institutes performing military research (TNO and Fraunhofer-Gesellschaft). Neither civil society nor the academic world was represented. The conclusion of the report of the GoP (EU Institute for Security Studies, 2016) was predictable and came down to the creation of a subsidy Fund for the arms industry of €3.5 billion. This recommendation was literally copied in the European Defence Action Plan, which the Commission published in November 2016.

The companies advising the European Commission in 2015–2016 turn out to be the biggest beneficiaries of the funds. To date, all but one of the eight[12] companies and research centres represented in the Group of Personalities are getting funding from the Preparatory Action on Defence Research. They participate in five of the current seven selected projects, and many of them participate in several projects in parallel (European Defence Agency, 2020a). Especially the Ocean2020 project stands out a project to develop surveillance drones and autonomous submarines. Six of the companies which were represented in the Group of Personalities participate in the Ocean2020 project, receiving in total close to €17 million (European Defence Agency, 2020b).

The conflict of interest at the heart of the European Defence Fund prompted the European Ombudsman, after a complaint from the European Network Against Arms Trade (ENAAT) about the lack of transparency of the Group of Personalities, to state that:

> Transparency in this regard should have been especially important in the case of the Group of Personalities given that companies represented within the group could be eligible for funding under the programmes that it was advising on. In fact, it is the case that companies represented within the group did subsequently receive such funding.
>
> (European Ombudsman, 2018)

5.6 Conclusion

Recent EU funding for the arms industry has been specifically designed to answer perceived military needs, from the point of view of both the industry and national governments. This occurred after a similar process was carried out in relation to the security sector. Chapter 2 describes how other policy areas are now asked to adapt human resources, infrastructure and technologies for military use or purposes. Several billions of euros are to be dedicated to the arms industry or to facilitate the movement of military troops and equipment.

External borders management and also some elements of external policies are increasingly considered through a security and military prism, including the provision of equipment and means, and receiving billions of Euros of tax-payers' money. And Chapter 4 gives us an insight into the role of the arms industry in shaping defence-related EU developments, to an extent that many will question the legitimacy of the decisions made.

Moreover, we have seen that under its security programmes the EU is starting to buy dual-use equipment on its own, and the European Defence Fund foresees the possibility of an EU 'technical' support to Member States' joint acquisition (European Commission, 2018a). Joint or collaborative pro-curement and acquisitions are set as key benchmarks for success, and the most ambitious scenario of the Commission on Defence contemplates «Common financing and procurement of capabilities supported by the EU budget» (European Commission, 2017d: 16). In light of the parallelism between pre-vious developments in the security sector and current ones in the military field, it seems reasonable to consider EU-funded military acquisitions as a credible option in the not-too-distant future under a Defence Union called for by 2025 (Juncker, 2017).

We can even go a step further: according to Andrew Bickford (2015) «[b]roadly defined, militarization is the cultural, symbolic, and material preparation for war, [...] Most importantly, militarization is an intentional process, something a state or group must set out to do».

EU developments are part of an intentional process, led by the European Commission and agreed by a majority of the final decision-makers, such as the European Parliament and national governments. They partly aim at providing advanced weaponry and military equipment to the EU member states and beyond. Intergovernmental initiatives under the EDA and PESCO framework also aim at strengthening member states' operational capacities, which is happening under a general rhetoric about security threats and about an 'existential need' for EU hard power and for an «EU that protects [...] and defends» (Juncker, 2016: 5).

The EU may be engaging in a political, industrial and material militari-sation of conflicts. By doing so, the EU is contributing to serious military spending increases and to the global arms race, a shift that might sideline and even work against the traditional EU support for alternative peace-building and for efforts to tackle root-causes of conflicts.

Notes

1 EU Budget 2015 – Section III – Item 02 04 77 02 – Pilot project – CSDP research, http://eur-lex.europa.eu/budget/data/General/2015/en/SEC03.pdf.
2 EU Budget 2017 – Section III – Item 02 04 77 03 – Preparatory Action for Defence Research, p. 515, https://eur-lex.europa.eu/legal-content/EN/TXT/PDF/?uri=OJ:L:2017:051:FULL&from=EN.

3 Provisional agreement on the European Defence Fund Regulation, April 2019, http://www.europarl.europa.eu/doceo/document/TA-8-2019-0430_EN.html? redirect.
4 This turned into a European Network of Defence-related Regions, which aims to support SMEs and entrepreneurs willing to develop defence and dual-use technologies, products and services, and facilitate their access to EU funding; https://www.endr.eu/about-us.
5 The table produced by the European Defence Agency in order to help companies access EU funding gives a clear picture of the wide scope of support, available at 'European Funding Gateway' https://www.eda.europa.eu/what-we-do/ eda-priorities/eu-funding-opportunities.
6 The concept of European Defence Union is still unclear; what the Commission has in mind refers mainly to market and industrial dimensions, such as harmonised procurement rules, an effective internal defence market including freedom of movement, more industrial cooperation and possibly joint acquisitions, as well as qualified majority voting at Council level. It does not refer to the setting-up of a European army. See fact-sheet 'Towards a European Defence Union', May 2019, https://ec.europa.eu/commission/sites/beta-political/files/euco-sibiu-towards_ a_european_defence_union_0.pdf.
7 It's named Alliance for Strategic Skills addressing Emerging Technologies in Defence, more information in https://eacea.ec.europa.eu/sites/eacea-site/files/ projects_list_ssa_2019_lot_3.pdf and it aims building «a sustainable human resources supply chain that allows defence sector companies to attract highly skilled workers and up-skill employees through customised, complementary education and training programmes in robotics, C4ISTAR and cybersecurity»EDSP webpage https://eu-ems.com/summary.asp?event_id=4370&page_id=9753.
8 Source data for this chapter has been previously published in Akkerman (2016a), Akkerman (2016b), Akkerman (2018).
9 Eurosur is a 'system of surveillance systems', which combines surveillance data of all member states into a continuous live picture of the situation at the EU external borders and beyond.
10 European Dactyloscopy (Eurodac) is the European Union (EU) fingerprint database for identifying asylum seekers and irregular border-crossers.
11 The idea was later cancelled due to pressure from budgetary conservative member states such as the Netherlands.
12 So far only BAE Systems is not involved in a PADR project. The ninth representative of the industry is the lobby group ASD, which is not active in industrial R&D.

Bibliography

Akkerman, Mark (2016a), *Border Wars: the arms dealers profiting from Europe's refugee tragedy*, Amsterdam: Stop Wapenhandel/TNI.
Akkerman, Mark (2016b), *Border Wars II: an update on the arms dealers profiting from Europe's refugee tragedy*, Amsterdam: Stop Wapenhandel/TNI.
Akkerman, Mark (2018), *Expanding the Fortress: the policies, the profiteers and the people shaped by EU's border externalisation programme*, Amsterdam: Stop Wapenhandel/TNI.
ASD (2016), Considerations on *'Capacity building in support of security and development (CBSD) in third countries'*, https://www.asd-europe.org/considerations-on -capacity-building-in-support-of-security-and-development-cbsd-in-third -countries, accessed 11 September 2019
Bartels, Hans-Peter, Anna Maria Kellener, and Uwe Optenhögel (2017), *Strategic autonomy and the defence of Europe – on the road to a european army?*, Bonn: Dietz.

Bickford, Andrew (2015), *Anthropology of militaries and militarisation*, in *International Encyclopedia of the Social & Behavioral Sciences* (Second Edition), 2015 https://www.sciencedirect.com/topics/social-sciences/militarization, accessed 20 August 2019

Bulc, Violeta (2018), Speech at the North Atlantic Council, https://europa.eu/rapid/press-release_SPEECH-18-4126_en.htm, accessed 12 September 2019

Buzan, Barry, Ole Wæver and Jaap de Wilde (1998), *Security: a new framework for analysis*, Boulder: Lynne Reinner.

CEO – Corporate Europe Observatory, (2008), *The silent bubble*, http://blog.brusselsbubble.eu/2008/12/silent-bubble.html

CEO – Corporate Europe Observatory (2011), '*Lobbying Warfare, the arms industry's role in building a military Europe*', September 2011, Brussels.

CEO – Corporate Europe Observatory (2019), Thierry Breton, the corporate commissioner?. https://corporateeurope.org/en/2019/11/thierry-breton-corporate-commissioner, accessed 5 May 2020

CONCORD-EPLO-HRDN-VOICE, (2018), Letter to the EU heads of State and Government, 20 June 2018, https://concordeurope.org/wp-content/uploads/2018/06/CONCORD-EPLO-HRDN-VOICE_JointLetter_MFF_June2018.pdf, accessed 25 May 2019

Convention for European Economic Cooperation (2013): Groupe de travail VIII «Défense », Rapport du Président du groupe de travail VIII « Défense » aux Membres de la Convention, CONV 461/02 – WG VIII 22, Bruxelles, 16.10.02

Council of the EU (2019), European Border and Coast Guard: Council confirms agreement on stronger mandate, press release, https://www.consilium.europa.eu/en/press/press-releases/2019/04/01/european-border-and-coast-guard-council-confirms-agreement-on-stronger-mandate, accessed 11 September 2019

De Correspondent, (2017), *Als de wapenlobby het vraagt, komt de Eurocommissaris opdraven*, https://decorrespondent.nl/6245/als-de-wapenlobby-het-vraagt-komt-de-eurocommissaris-opdraven/1381856392290-e433c3ad, accessed 11 September 2019

Deutsche Welle (2017), Merkel calls for greater investment in Africa ahead of G20 summit, https://www.dw.com/en/merkel-calls-for-greater-investment-in-africa-ahead-of-g20-summit/a-39220029, accessed 11 September 2019

Eisenhower, Dwight (1961): *Farewell address delivered 17 January 1961, available at American Rethoric:* https://americanrhetoric.com/speeches/dwightdeisenhowerfarewell.html, accessed 18 January 2020

Emmott, Robin (2019), 'EU creates defence and space branch 'to complement NATO'https://mobile-reuters-com.cdn.ampproject.org/c/s/mobile.reuters.com/-article/amp/idUSKCN1VV1CX, accessed 12 September 2019

EU Institute for Security Studies (2016), *Report of the group of personalities on the preparatory action for CSDP-related research European defence research, the case for an EU-funded defence R&T programme*, EUISS, Paris.

European Commission (2011), Eurosur: Providing authorities with tools needed to reinforce management of external borders and fight cross-border crime, press release, http://www.emsa.europa.eu/news-a-press-centre/other-press-releases/item/1358-eurosur-providing-authorities-with-tools-needed-to-reinforce-management-of-external-borders-and-fight-cross-border-crime.html, accessed 11 September 2019

European Commission (2013), Communication from the European Commission to the European Parliament and the Council, *"Towards a more competitive and efficient defence and security sector"*, COM(2013) 542 final.

European Commission (2016), Communication from the Commission, *'European Defence Action Plan'* COM(2016) 950 final.

European Commission (2017a), Proposal for a regulation of the European Parliament and of the Council, *Establishing the European Defence Industrial Development Programme aiming at supporting the competitiveness and innovative capacity of the EU defence industry,* COM(2017) 294 final.

European Commission (2017b), Communication for the European Commission, *Launching the European Defence Fund,* COM(2017) 295 final.

European Commission (2017c), Fact-sheet, *blue print for sectoral cooperation on skills,* https://ec.europa.eu/docsroom/documents/21726

European Commission (2017d), *Reflection paper on the future of European defence.* COM(2017) 315 final

European Commission (2018a), Proposal for a regulation of the European parliament and of the council, *Establishing the European Defence Fund,* COM(2018) 476 final.

European Commission (2018b), *Joint communication to the European Parliament and the Council on the action plan on military mobility,* JOIN(2018) 5 final.

European Commission (2018c), Evaluation of the Regulation (EU) No 1052/2013 of the European Parliament and of the Council of 22 October 2013 establishing the European Border Surveillance System (Eurosur), Commission Staff Working Document, SWD(2018) 410 final, Brussels.

European Commission (2020), Skills in the defence sector, available at EC DG Growth website: https://ec.europa.eu/growth/sectors/defence/skills_en

European Defence Agency (2007), "Solana, Verheugen, Svensson at EDA Conference – Radical Change and True European Market Needed to Secure Future of European Defence Industry", available in European Defence Agency website: https://-www.eda.europa.eu/info-hub/press-centre/latest-news/2007/01/31/Solana _Verheugen_Svensson_at_EDA_Conference_-_Radical_Change_and_True _European_Market_Needed_to_Secure_Future_of_European_Defence_Industry, accessed 14 September 2019

European Defence Agency (2020a), "Open cooperation for European mAritime awareNess (OCEAN2020)", European Defence Agency Website: https://www.eda. europa.eu/docs/default-source/documents/padr-ocean2020-projectweb_v3.pdf

European Defence Agency (2020b), *Pilot project and preparatory action on defence research,* European Defence Agency Website: https://eda.europa.eu/what-we-do/ activities/activities-search/pilot-project-and-preparatory-action-for-defence-research, accessed 7 April 2020

European Ombudsman (2018), Decision in case 811/2017/EA on the transparency of "advisory bodies" that influence the development of EU policy, European Ombudsman Website: https://www.ombudsman.europa.eu/en/decision/en/103874, accessed 14 September 2019

European Parliament (2019), Revised EU approach to security and development funding (Instrument contributing to Stability and Peace), http://www.europarl. europa.eu/legislative-train/theme-europe-as-a-stronger-global-actor/file-revised-eu-approach-to-security-and-development-funding, accessed 11 September 2019

Fischer-Lescano, Andreas (2018) *Legal opinion on the illegality of the European defence fund,* Bremen: Faculty of Law, University of Bremen.

Frontex (2019), Explanatory note to the Management Board on the Comprehensive strategy for the acquisition and lease of Frontex own technical equipment – revised strategic considerations, Management board meeting on 22 January 2019 in Warsaw, agenda point 9.1.

Gros-Verheyde, Nicolas (2018) *European army: no longer a taboo subject*, Euractiv https://www.euractiv.com/section/politics/news/european-army-no-longer-a-taboo-subject/, accessed 20 August 2019

Hayes, Ben (2009), *NeoConOpticon: the EU security-industrial complex*, Amsterdam/London: Transnational Institute and Statewatch.

James, Andrew D. (2018), Policy entrepreneurship and agenda setting: comparing and contrasting the origins of the European research programmes for security and defence In Nikolaos karampekios, Iraklis Oikonomou and Elias G. Carayannis (2018), *The Emergence of EU Defense Research Policy: From Innovation to Militarization*, Springer, P. 15–43.

Jones, Chris (2017), *Market forces: The development of the EU security-industrial complex*, Amsterdam/London: Statewatch and TNI.

Juncker, Jean-Claude (2017), *State of the union address*.

Karampekios, Nikolaos Oikonomou, Iraklis and Carayannis, Elias G. (Eds) (2018), *The emergence of EU defense research policy: from innovation to militarization*, Springer, Cham

Kluth, Michael Friederich (2009), *Cross border EU defence industry consolidation between globalization and europeanization*. Paper presented at ISA Annual Convention: Exploring the past, anticipating the future, New York, United States

Lobbyfacts (2019): Statistics, available in Website Lobbyfacts.eu, https://lobbyfacts.eu/reports/lobby-costs/all, accessed 29 August 2019

Oikonomou, Iraklis (2008), The internationalization of the European arms industry: trends and implications, *Agora Without Frontiers* Volume 13 (4), p. 362–375.

Politico, (22/12/17), *Brussels influence, conscientious objectors — open up, Mr. Tusk — Agency report card*, https://www.politico.eu/newsletter/politico-eu-influence/politico-brussels-influence-presented-by-plastics-recyclers-europe-conscientious-objectors-open-up-mr-tusk-agency-report-card/, accessed 11 September 2019

Slijper, Frank (2005), *The emerging EU Military-Industrial Complex – arms industry lobbying in Brussels*, Amsterdam: TNI.

Teffer, Peter (2018), *Rise of killer robots seems inevitable at EU conference*, EU Observer, https://euobserver.com/science/143546, accessed 11 September 2019

Valero, Jorge (2019), *The Brief – Von der Leyen needs to prove she won't be Barroso III*, https://www.euractiv.com/section/future-eu/news/the-brief-von-der-leyen-needs-to-prove-she-wont-be-barroso-iii/, accessed 16 September 2019

von der Leyen, Ursula (2019), Mission letter to Thierry Breton, Commissioner-Designate for Internal Market, https://ec.europa.eu/commission/sites/beta-political/files/president-elect_von_der_leyens_mission_letter_to_thierry_breton.pdf, accessed 20 November 2019

Vranken, Bram (2017), *Securing profits: how the arms lobby is hijacking Europe's defence policy*, Berchem: Vredesactie.

6 Cost of nuclear weapons

Tarja Cronberg and Dave Webb

6.1 Introduction

How much are we prepared to spend on weapons that can never be used? Before he became president, Donald Trump was reported as asking three times during a briefing on foreign affairs 'If we have nuclear weapons why can't we use them?' (Allen, Lawler and Sherlock, 2016) although this report was later denied by Trump's team it does pose important questions – what are the costs of nuclear weapons and are they worth it? In the past, the existence of nuclear weapons has been justified by the security paradigm of deterrence and 'Mutually Assured Destruction'. Nuclear deterrence is about beliefs and credible threats, not about implementing the nuclear option. What policy-makers want, after all, is what they can get from the threat value of a nuclear weapon, not what they can get from actually carrying out a nuclear strike (Schell, 2017). However, this may not be the case for all politicians and members of the military, some had considered and even lobbied for a full scale first strike surprise attack which could give an advantage to the United States. However, calculations showed that it would still mean massive casualties on both sides (Kaplan, 2001).

Consequently, when it is claimed that nuclear weapons have not been used for the past 70 years it means only that no nuclear bombs have been dropped or missiles fired by one nation against another – the threat dimension of these weapons is in use every day. Sometimes this has been clearly expressed by the threatening statements or behaviour directed against an adversary, as described by Joseph Gerson (2007) in his book *Empire and the Bomb*. At other times it has been symbolised by placing missiles on hair-trigger alert.

As the value of nuclear weapons is essentially a threat value, it seems amazing that nuclear weapon states are able to carry the costs of actually building these weapons and the public accepts this expenditure even at the same time as they experience damaging cuts in the provision of welfare and education. At the end of the Cold War there was an engaged discussion about a 'peace dividend' – money that could now be spent on education or health instead of the arms race and development of new weapons. However, this dividend did not materialise. In fact it turned out that the destruction of weapons under arms control agreements was much more expensive than building new ones. Today, there is a new discussion on the need and possibility to finance the prevention of climate change with the money now spent on nuclear weapons. In this way mankind could avoid two catastrophic scenarios for the price of one. In this chapter we look at the amount of money spent by each nuclear weapons state and show how nuclear expenditure is securitised outside the normal political processes – see, for example, Taureck (2006).

6.2 The full costs of nuclear weapons

To quote Harrington de Santana (2009) 'nuclear weapons function as the currency of power in the international system' and, by looking closely at the costs of these weapons, we want to raise the basic question of whether the costs and benefits actually balance. Nuclear weapons, as threat producers, are extremely expensive because the cost of their maintenance alone, not to mention the ongoing modernisation efforts, represent resources not available for fighting poverty or climate change. Besides, it is important to realise that the usual quotes about the costs of nuclear weapons just concern the costs of the weapons systems themselves. The cost of producing the weapons grade materials and of the support infrastructure is usually not included. The extra expenditure required to support a nuclear arsenal also includes maintenance costs of submarines, bombers and launch silos. Furthermore, there are military security costs (guarding the weapons and associated installations), transport costs, the costs of compensation for test victims, research and development costs, to name a few. In addition, there are a large number of personnel working in laboratories, military bases and installations that need to be supported to keep the nuclear weapons programmes going. None of this is usually accounted for. Therefore, if the effects of cost overruns and the infrastructure costs are also included, then the final figures for the overall costs of nuclear weapons will be significantly higher than the numbers discussed below.

To appreciate the scale of the infrastructure needed to support a nuclear weapons programme, it is instructive to consider the initial costs, shown in Table 6.3, of the *Manhattan Project*, the secret US wartime project that first developed the bomb at Los Alamos. The *Comprehensive Test Ban Treaty Organisation* has described how the project grew from a small research experiment in 1939 to eventually employ more than 130,000 people at an estimated cost of nearly $2 billion -equivalent to about $28 billion in 2018 inflation corrected dollars (CTBTO, n.d.).

A breakdown of the costs incurred by the development of the sites constructed for the project up to the end of 1945 shows the extent of the infrastructure required for its initial and continuing development. Oak Ridge was established as a pilot reactor to produce plutonium from highly enriched uranium and the plutonium used in the bombs was produced at the Hanford Engineering Works.

Table 6.1 Itemised costs of Manhattan Project

Site/Project	1945 dollars	%
Establishing the Oak Ridge National Laboratory		
K-25 Gaseous Diffusion Plant	$ 512,166,000	27
Y-12 Electromagnetic Plant	$ 477,631,000	25
Clinton Engineer Works, HQ and central utilities	$ 155,951,000	8
Clinton Laboratories	$ 26,932,000	1
S-50 Thermal Diffusion Plant	$ 15,672,000	1
Oak Ridge total	$ 1,188,352,000	63
Hanford engineering works	$ 390,124,000	21
Special operating materials	$ 103,369,000	5
Los Alamos Project	$ 74,055,000	4
Research and development	$ 69,681,000	4
Government overhead	$ 37,255,000	2
Heavy water plants	$ 26,768,000	1
Grand total	$1,889,604,000	

Source: own elaboration.

Following the first test of a nuclear bomb by the Soviet Union in 1949, the US government claimed that nuclear weapons were a relatively inexpensive way of ensuring a state of '*Mutually Assured Destruction*' that would prevent a nuclear war from happening. Therefore, little attention was paid to the escalating costs of the US nuclear weapons programme. That is, until 1998 when Stephen Schwartz published his *Atomic Audit* which concluded that the United States had manufactured and deployed more than 70,000 nuclear weapons and spent $5 trillion from 1940 to 1998 on developing and maintaining its nuclear arsenal. This is equivalent to $69.75 trillion in 2018 dollars. However, there is a large degree of uncertainty on this figure. As mentioned above and as Schwartz himself notes:

> The problem is not […] that the government 'has never officially disclosed the exact cost', it's that no one knows the exact cost because all the relevant data have never been collected and analysed.
>
> (Schwartz, 1998)

In a 2008 follow-up article in *Nuclear Files*, Schwartz points out (see Figure 6.1) that the largest portion of the costs ($3.2 trillion or 56% of the total) are incurred by the provision of the delivery systems – aircraft, missiles, submarines, etc. It is difficult to appreciate exactly what these numbers mean but as an illustration, counting out $1 trillion at the rate of $1 per second would take 31,709 years, so you would need 184,579 years of free time to count out $5.8 trillion!

A further study by Cirincione (2005) using the same methods as the *Atomic Audit* found that total costs at that time were $7.5 trillion in adjusted 2005 $ (equivalent to $9.6 trillion in 2018 $).

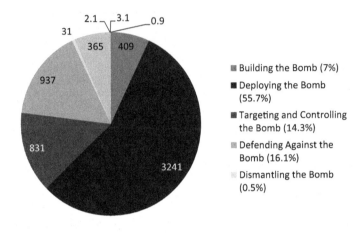

Total cost: $5,821 billion

Figure 6.1 Estimated minimum incurred costs of US Nuclear Weapons Programs, 1940–1998.

Source: own elaboration based on Schwartz (2008).

6.3 The nuclear arsenals and their costs

Today there are around 14,000 nuclear weapons in the world. Although this is more than enough to threaten all life on Earth, it is a considerable reduction on the 70,300 reached in 1986 at the height of the Cold War (Kristensen and Korda, 2019a). The United States and Russia together are responsible for over 90% of the world's nuclear arsenals and the distribution of the rest is as shown in Table 6.2.

The most recent estimates of world military spending on nuclear weapons are shown in Table 6.3. These estimates were made by Cramer (2009) and Blair and Brown (2011) for the Global Zero Campaign. According to Blair and Brown, the estimated annual expenditure on nuclear weapons worldwide in 2011 was around $105 billion. This was an increase of some $15 billion over 2008 and 2010 spending and is equivalent to about $12 million an hour.

In 2010 nuclear weapons spending was more than twice the official development assistance provided to Africa and equal to the gross domestic product of Bangladesh, a nation with a population of around 160 million. The entire core budget of the UN is around $5 billion per annum – about the same as the annual expenditure on nuclear weapons by the United Kingdom, France or India. The UN Office for Disarmament Affairs, which aims to achieve the ultimate goal of general and complete disarmament, has an annual budget of $10 million, which is less than the amount spent on nuclear weapons every hour.

The nuclear weapon states have never comprehensively tracked and accounted for all of the related spending on nuclear weapons and so the figures

Table 6.2 Nine nuclear states have around 14,000 nuclear weapons

Country	Deployed warheads	Other warheads	Total inventory
United States	1,750	4,435	6,185
Russia	1,600	4,900	6,500
United Kingdom	120	80	200
France	280	20	300
China	–	290	290
India	–	130–140	130–140
Pakistan	–	150–160	150–160
Israel	–	80–90	80–90
North Korea	–	(20–30)	(20–30)
Total	3,750	10,115	13,865

Source: own elaboration from SIPRI (2019).

Table 6.3 Estimated annual expenditure on nuclear weapons

Country	2008 spending (in billions of $)	2010 spending (in billions of $)	2011 spending (in billions of $)
United States	52–55	55.6	61.3
Russia	6–7	9.7	14.8
China	10.0	6.8	7.6
France	6.5–7	5.9	6.0
United Kingdom	6–7	4.5	5.5
India	3.0–3.5	4.1	4.9
Israel	1.5	1.9	1.9
Pakistan	1.1	1.8	2.2
North Korea	1.0	0.7	0.7
Total	87.1–93.1	91.0	104.9

Source: IPB (2008) and Global Zero (2010 & 2011).
Note: Figures in US dollars.

shown in Table 6.2 are likely to be underestimates. The actual expenses will be much higher as the total cost will be spread over a number of different departments with some expenses, such as the running costs of nuclear infrastructure, compensation for test victims, secret radiation experiments, etc., not accounted for or even adequately documented.

Full figures have therefore not been made available on a regular basis and to determine the true overall cost requires taking into account the costs of production, delivery systems and maintenance. In addition, information on the size and status of the nuclear arsenals and their capabilities, is also difficult to obtain, leading to a wide range of estimates being made. As Stockholm International Peace Research Institute (SIPRI) has pointed out:

> The USA and the UK have disclosed considerable information about their respective nuclear stockpiles and capabilities, and France has also declared some information. Russia refuses to publicly disclose a detailed

breakdown of its forces counted under New START, even though it shares this information with the USA. China now publicly displays its nuclear forces more frequently than in the past but releases little information about force numbers or future development plans. The governments of India and Pakistan make statements about some of their missile tests but provide no information about the status or size of their arsenals. North Korea has acknowledged conducting nuclear weapon and missile tests but provides no information about its nuclear weapon capabilities. Israel has a long-standing policy of not commenting on its nuclear arsenal.

(SIPRI, 2019)

6.4 The 'modernisation' process

The cost of nuclear weapons is not only about maintaining the existing weapons. Currently, all nuclear states, except perhaps North Korea who have only just developed a first generation of nuclear weapons, are 'modernising' (really upgrading) their nuclear arsenals. New low-yield bombs and warheads are being developed, which are classed as 'more usable' and are expected to lower the threshold for their use. The upgrades that are generating the most concern are those of the three great powers: the United States, Russia and China. The relative decline of US global power, China's economic and now military rise, and the re-emergence of an assertive Russia mean that the triangular strategic relationship between these three will have an enormous effect on global peace and security (Zala, 2019). However, it is not only the superpowers who are modernising their arsenals. France and the United Kingdom are two nuclear weapon states whose weapons are not directly a response to a security threat but rather an insurance policy for the future (Cronberg, 2010), and they are also upgrading their systems and calling the process 'modernisation'. Nuclear weapons upgrades are going on even in states outside the Nuclear Non-Proliferation Treaty – i.e. India, Pakistan and Israel.

These 'modernisation' policies will generate huge costs. For example, the US policy agreed to during the Obama administration is expected to reach 1.2–1.4 billion during 2017–2046 (CBO, 2017b). It should also be remembered that 'modernisation' not only implies the costs of the weapons arsenals but will also entail additional associated technologies such as missile defence systems, anti-satellite and anti-submarine weapons, and precision-strike missile technology, as well as cutting-edge cyber and artificial intelligence capabilities – all of which are aimed at reducing the vulnerability of the nuclear weapon states to first strike or retaliatory attacks. Full details of the costs of all of these upgrades and their complementary costs are not freely available. There is however, some detailed information about the United States, United Kingdom and French arsenals and the government expenditure involved. It is instructive to look at these as examples of what is involved.

6.4.1 The US nuclear arsenal

US nuclear forces consist of submarine launched ballistic missiles (SLBMs), land-based intercontinental ballistic missiles (ICBMs), long-range bomber aircraft, shorter-range tactical aircraft carrying bombs and the nuclear war-heads that those delivery systems carry. All of these are to be upgraded, refurbished or replaced with new systems in the next 20 years.

The US Congressional Budget Office (CBO) is required to project the ten-year costs of nuclear forces every two years. Its report issued in February 2017 (CBO, 2017a) estimated the total cost of US nuclear forces from 2017 to 2026 at $400 billion. This was $52 billion, or 15%, more than its January 2015 estimate of $348 billion for the 2015–2024 period. The Department of Defence's (DoD's) costs were projected to be $267 billion (some 18% higher than estimated in 2015), whereas the Department of Energy's (DoE's) costs were projected to total $134 billion (11% higher estimated in 2015).

However, in October 2017 the CBO issued a report on the rising cost of plans to sustain and upgrade US nuclear forces. Entitled 'Approaches for Managing the Cost of U.S. Nuclear Forces, 2017 to 2046' (CBO, 2017b), it warned of the challenges that the current plans faced. It came at a time when the Trump administration's Nuclear Posture Review (NPR) was call-ing for an increase in the role of nuclear weapons in US defence policy. President Trump made it clear that he would like to 'strengthen and expand' US nuclear capabilities. Writing in the *Guardian* newspaper, Borger (2017) reported that the US administration was considering options to bolster the nuclear arsenal and make it 'more usable'. These plans include the introduc-tion of lower-yield warheads for US ballistic missiles, a re-nuclearisation of the Tomahawk sea-launched cruise missile, and a reduction in the amount of time it would take to resume nuclear explosive testing.

The CBO estimated that the nuclear weapons spending plans would cost $1.2 trillion in inflation-adjusted dollars between 2017 and 2046. This is equivalent to about 6% of the expected national defence spending for the same period. Three hundred ninety-nine billion dollars of the $1.2 trillion would be allocated for acquiring new missiles, bombers and submarines and conducting W-80 nuclear warhead and B61-12 atomic bomb life-extension programmes. The remaining $843 billion would be used for maintaining existing forces and the new ones, following their entry into service. Annual costs are expected to peak at $50 billion in the late 2020s and early 2030s, during which time, they would account for about 8% of total national defence spending and 15% of the Defence Department's acquisition costs.

The CBO's projections for 2019–2028 were presented in January 2019 and budget requests from the DoD and the DOE are estimated to total some $494 billion for the period 2019–2028, at an average of just under $50 billion a year – in line with their October 2017 predictions for 2017–2046 (CBO, 2019). This represents a 23% increase in the CBO's 2017 estimate of the ten-year costs and $400 billion more than the 2017–2026 period. Around

$37 billion (or 39%) of the $94 billion increase is expected to occur from 2019 to 2026 and comes mainly from new weapons upgrading programmes and plans for nuclear command-and-control systems.

If the effects of inflation are included, Reif (2017) predicted that the 30-year cost would be more like $1.7 trillion, significantly higher than previously reported estimates of roughly $1 trillion. A full detailed costing of the US programme has been presented by Kristensen and Korda (2019b).

However, these are not the total costs of the US nuclear weapons programme. The CBO has not included the clean-up of nuclear weapons sites in their figures. These legacy costs are likely to add another $541 billion to the overall bill for the US nuclear arsenal (Alvarez, 2018). Of this, $179.5 billion is needed for the storage and disposal of the high-level radioactive waste generated by the production of plutonium. In 2013 the US Government Accountability Office (GAO) informed Congress that these are 'considered one of the most hazardous substances on earth'. Therefore, the total US costs rise to an astonishing $2.24 trillion. So, the average annual cost of US nuclear weapons will be at least $74.7 billion over 30 years.

6.4.2 The UK nuclear weapons system

The United Kingdom decommissioned its tactical WE.177 bombs in 1998 and currently has one nuclear weapons delivery system, consisting of four *Vanguard* class nuclear submarines based in Faslane in Scotland. At least one submarine is always on patrol, providing a continuous at-sea deterrent role. Each submarine is armed with up to 16 US Trident II missiles, each of which is capable of carrying up to eight multiple independently targetable re-entry vehicles (MIRVs) produced jointly by the United States (at Sandia National Laboratories) and the United Kingdom (at the Atomic Weapons Research Establishment in Aldermaston, Berkshire). A full detail of the development of UK nuclear weapons has been presented by Norris and Kristensen (2013).

In September 2010, the UK government announced that it had 'not more than 225' Trident nuclear warheads and that this would be reduced to 'not more than 180' by the mid-2020s (HMG, 2010a). One hundred twenty of these warheads were 'operationally available' in January 2015. The warheads are manufactured and assembled at the Atomic Weapons Establishment (AWE) facilities at Burghfield, Berkshire and are transported to the storage depot 450 miles away at Coulport in Scotland by heavily guarded convoys. The United Kingdom has access to US warhead design under the 1958 US–UK Mutual Defence Agreement, but their construction and maintenance is carried out at the AWE. Kristensen (2006) has argued that the British nuclear warhead is based on the design of the US W76 warhead, which the MoD eventually admitted. The Trident warhead's fusing, arming and firing mechanisms were upgraded in 2016/2017 to provide greater accuracy and lethality.

The UK parliament agreed to upgrade the Trident system in 2007 and 'conceptual' work on potential designs for replacement submarines, propulsion systems and other key components began. The 'Initial Gate' phase, consisting of £3bn in procurement of important items, was approved in 2011 and the ultimate decision on whether to proceed and how many submarines to order was delayed but eventually agreed in 2016. The new system will be based on a new *Dreadnought* class of nuclear submarines, carrying upgraded US missiles. The delivery date for the first submarine has been put back to 2028.

In 2019, the UK government issued figures on the costs of the *Dreadnought* nuclear submarine system (House of Commons Library, 2019). These consisted of £31 billion for the cost of manufacture of submarines (HMG, 2015) plus a contingency fund of £10 billion (35% of the submarine cost) – representing a total of £41 billion. So far, the Ministry of Defence (MoD) has spent £5.5 billion on the programme and has accessed £600 million of the contingency.

However, an estimate of the total costs of replacing and running *Dreadnought* through its 25 year intended lifetime have been issued by the UK *Campaign for Nuclear Disarmament* (CND, 2016). These are itemised as follows:

- Manufacturing four successor submarines – £31 billion
- Contingency fund – £10 billion
- Missile extension programme – £350 million
- Replacement warheads – £4 billion
- Infrastructure capital costs – £4 billion
- In service costs – £142 billion
- Conventional forces directly assigned to support Trident – £1 billion
- Decommissioning – £13 billion.

Total – £205 billion or £8.2 billion per year over 25 years.

This figure gives a more realistic view of how much it costs to maintain and operate even a nuclear weapons system considered to be relatively small. So, the average annual cost of UK nuclear weapons will be around $10.3 billion over 25 years.

6.4.3 The French nuclear arsenal

France's nuclear stockpile has remained at approximately 300 warheads in recent years, but significant upgrading is underway with regard to ballistic missiles, cruise missiles, submarines, aircraft and the nuclear industrial complex (Kristensen and Korda, 2019c).

SLBMs are at the centre of the French nuclear arsenal and the French Navy operates four *Triomphant*-class nuclear-powered ballistic missile submarines equipped with nuclear-armed long-range ballistic missiles. The French Navy also maintains a continuous at-sea deterrent posture with at least one boat on patrol. Each submarine can carry 16 M51 SLBMs, but since one boat is always undergoing routine maintenance, France has only produced enough missiles for three boats.

The M51.1 missile can carry up to six 100-kiloton TN75 MIRV warheads, but probably only carries an average of five. An upgraded version of the warhead, the M51.2, was declared operational in December 2017 by Florence Parly, the French Minister of the Armed Forces (Parly, 2017). One submarine has also been upgraded to carry a new warhead, the *tête nucléaire océanique*, or TNO, which is housed in a new re-entry vehicle (Kile and Kristensen, 2017). The remaining submarines are due to be upgraded to the M51.2 by 2020 and a third version, the M51.3, is scheduled for completion by 2025. The development of a new generation of ballistic missile submarine (known as SNLE-3G) is expected to begin during the period 2019–2025 and to enter into service around 2035.

The second component of the French nuclear arsenal involves nuclear ASMPA cruise missiles delivered by fighter-bombers operated by the Strategic Air Forces (with two squadrons of 40 nuclear-capable Rafale BF3 aircraft) and the Naval Nuclear Aviation Force (with one or two squadrons of 11 or 12 Rafale MF3 aircraft deployed on the *Charles de Gaulle* aircraft carrier). In April 2018 France and Germany announced that they would jointly develop a sixth-generation combat aircraft that could potentially be nuclear-capable. The Rafales have a relatively short range and so a fleet of refuelling aircraft is needed to support them. Currently this consists of Boeing C-135FR and KC-135R tanker aircraft. Delivery of a fleet of 15 Airbus A330-200 'Phénix' Multi-Role Tanker Transport aircraft has been scheduled for completion by 2023.

France has begun design development of a stealthier, extended-range replacement for the ASMPA, which will be called the ASN4G and enter into service around 2035. Hypersonic technologies are among the potential ASN4G propulsion options, although this might increase the length of the missile beyond what the current Rafale aircraft can carry.

Florence Parly (2018) has also declared that between 2019 and 2023 the French Government will spend €25 billion on its nuclear forces – equivalent to $6.9 billion per year but this figure does not include decommissioning or clean-up costs. Full detailed costs of the French programme have been presented by Kristensen and Korda (2019c).

So, the average annual cost of French nuclear weapons will be at least $7 billion over at least four years.

Comparing the above figures of nuclear weapons expenditure for the United States, United Kingdom and France in Table 6.4, we see that the figures for the United Kingdom show a relatively higher increase than the others – this is because the UK figures (produced by CND) include more of the major infrastructure costs. These will actually be lower for the United Kingdom than for other countries as some of its costs are shared with the United States and France. The UK Trident missiles are leased from the United States and so there are no R&D costs and the warheads are developed together with the United States, and some costs and facilities are also shared with France under the 2010 *Tuetates* and other agreements (see, for example, HMG, 2010a).

Table 6.4 Comparative cost of nuclear weapon upgrades

Country	2011 Spending ($ billion)	Upgrade spending p.a. ($ billion)	No. of years
United States	61.3	74.7	30
United Kingdom	5.5	10.3	25
France	6.0	7	4

Source: own elaboration.

Although we do not have the same kind of detail about spending for the other nuclear states, it would probably be reasonable to assume that their costs will also be increasing in line with their 'modernisation' programmes and that any official figures are unlikely to include all of the infrastructure costs. Even the costs that we have managed to obtain some details of are not completely transparent and there are also other associated costs that should be considered to give a true picture.

6.5 Humanitarian costs

Humanitarian costs are rarely included in any weapons audit, but many people have suffered from their production, testing and use. Many of those affected were innocent victims who have never been provided with sufficient medical treatment or compensation – it is often difficult to prove that a victim's condition is the result of uranium mining, working in the nuclear industry or of nuclear tests. Humanitarian costs are also extremely difficult to quantify, and any money that is paid out cannot fully compensate for the hardships, suffering and pain inflicted on victims, their family and friends. However, some compensation schemes have been established in some countries.

Among those that received some recognition and medical aid are the survivors of the two atomic bombs dropped on Japan by the United States in 1945. It is an important acknowledgement of their mental and physical suffering that they were given a dominant voice by the International Campaign to Abolish Nuclear Weapons (ICAN) in the process of establishing the Treaty on the Prohibition of Nuclear Weapons in 2017.

6.5.1 The Hibakusha – survivors of Hiroshima and Nagasaki

There are various estimates of the number of people killed by the bombings of Hiroshima and Nagasaki, but an Appeal from Hiroshima and Nagasaki to the Third Special Session of the UN General Assembly on Devoted to Disarmament in 1988 stated that five months after the bombs were dropped around 210,000 people had died. At that time, there was little knowledge about the long-term effects of radiation and the Atomic Bomb Casualty Commission (ABCC) was set up in 1947 by President Truman to study them. Although the ABCC performed medical examinations of the *hibakusha* (the survivors of the Hiroshima and Nagasaki bombings), it did not provide medical treatment. This was extremely controversial and eventually led to the ABCC being disbanded in 1975.

Most of health problems of the *hibakusha* were not covered by Japanese health care laws, and the terms of the 1951 San Francisco Peace Treaty prevented them from suing the United States, so a fund-raising campaign and a legal movement to provide governmental support for *was set up*. The Atomic Bomb Victims Medical Care Law was finally established in 1957 and provided some benefits, but there were strict restrictions on eligibility, and it was not until 1995 that the Hibakusha Relief Law was passed (Atomic Heritage Foundation, 2017). Under this law, the Japanese government recognises *hibakusha* as those who were within 2 kms of the hypocentres of the bombings within two weeks of the bombings, were exposed to fallout, or not born at the time but carried by pregnant women in any of those categories. The government recognised about 650,000 people as *hibakusha* and, as of March 31, 2019, *Japan News* (2019) reported that 145,844 were still alive.

In 2003 a *Summary of Relief Measures for Atomic Bomb Survivors* (Hiroshima for Global Peace, 2003) indicated that between the years 1999 and 2003 the Japanese government paid $6.89 billion for health care for atomic bomb survivors, an average of $1.38 billion every year. This expenditure is decreasing as the numbers of *hibakusha* decrease and, although perhaps insignificant compared with the annual costs of the nuclear weapons systems it demonstrates the extent of the damage and suffering already caused by the use of two nuclear bombs which are small compared with most in today's arsenals. This is also an example of how some states are forced to take on some of the costs of the development or use of nuclear weapons by others.

6.5.2 Nuclear weapons tests

Environmental and health effects and compensation costs are also not normally included in any of the published nuclear weapons budgets. A General Overview of the effects of nuclear testing has been published on the website of the CTBTO. In the 1950s there were widespread public protests about the effects of nuclear weapons testing in the atmosphere and concerns about strontium-90 and its effect on mother's milk and babies' teeth. These led finally to the 1963 Partial Test Ban Treaty (PTBT), which banned nuclear testing in the atmosphere, outer space and under water, but not underground. It was signed by the United States, the Soviet Union and the United Kingdom. France and China did not sign and continued with atmospheric tests but eventually stopped in 1974 and 1980 respectively. A report by the United Nations Scientific Committee on the Effects of Atomic Radiation (UNSCEAR) to the General Assembly states that:

> The main man-made contribution to the exposure of the world's population [to radiation] has come from the testing of nuclear weapons in

the atmosphere, from 1945 to 1980. Each nuclear test resulted in unrestrained release into the environment of substantial quantities of radioactive materials, which were widely dispersed in the atmosphere and deposited everywhere on the Earth's surface.

(UNSCEAR, 2000)

On the ground, large areas of the planet have been made uninhabitable after nuclear testing, not only in states that have nuclear weapons, but also in others. This applies particularly to islands in the Pacific Ocean used for nuclear tests by the United States, Britain and France (see, for example, Ruff, 2015).

The total explosive power of US nuclear test explosions at the Nevada Test Site (on the land of the Western Shoshone people) was around 1.05 megatons (Mt) and affected the health of many people living nearby known as the 'Downwinders' (Taylor, 2018). The United States also dropped 152.8 Mt of bombs on islands in the Pacific – Bikini and Enewetak Atolls in the Marshall Islands, Johnston Atoll in the central Pacific Ocean, and Kiritimati (Christmas Island[1]). Following lengthy campaigns conducted by uranium workers and Downwinders, including the compilation of examples of health defects, a Radiation Exposure Compensation Act (RECA) was finally passed by the US government in 1990. Compensation under the act ranges from lump sums of $100,000 for uranium workers to $50,000 for those who lived downwind of the Nevada Test Site but current campaigns are working to increase the maximum payment to $150,000 and include victims downwind of *Trinity,* the first ever nuclear test in New Mexico in 1945. Over $2 billion in compensation had been approved under the act by 2015. Medical or other benefits are not provided by the RECA programme. However, uranium workers may be eligible for an additional $50,000 in compensation and benefits that pay for all medical costs associated with their illnesses covered under Part B of the Energy Employees Occupational Illness Compensation Program Act (EEOICPA).

The Soviet Union also created severe environmental and health problems through nuclear testing. From October 1961 to October 1989 they conducted 224 tests in Semipalatinsk's Degelen Mountain in Kazhakhstan and, in a statement to the UN in October 1998, Akmaral Kh. Arystanbekova, Permanent Representative of the Republic of Kazakhstan. spoke of the:

> severe socio-economic, humanitarian and ecological consequences, and also the serious harm by the negative impact to the environment of the many years of nuclear tests [by the Soviet Union] at the Semipalatinsk nuclear testing ground… The underground tests destroyed ecological linkages, and this in turn accelerated the process of desertification of the territory of the region, which is continuing to take place up until the present time. Large areas of land and water resources were subjected to radiation contamination, and economic activity in the territory located around the testing ground was considerably reduced.

(CTBTO, n.d.)

Nuclear tests have been held responsible for the many genetic defects and illnesses in the region, ranging from cancers to impotency to birth defects and other deformities. Many years later, Russia did offer some compensation to veterans of the 1954 Totsk test. It was conducted in Orenburg Oblast, Russia to train troops responding to a nuclear attack. However, there was no compensation to any civilians who suffered ill health from the test. Anti-nuclear groups say there has been no government compensation for other nuclear tests.

Britain carried out seven nuclear tests at Maralinga in South Australia between 1956 and 1957. Many of the indigenous population were moving around the region at the time of the tests. Little attention was paid to the vulnerability of these people to the effects of the tests. The contamination of their food, language barriers (many could not read the English warning signs) and general health status rendered them particularly susceptible to the effects of nuclear testing. After many years of campaigning by the victims and their representatives, the Australian government announced in 1986 that they would pay AU$500,000 (US$330,000) to indigenous populations in compensation for the contamination of their land by British nuclear tests. They also paid the Maralinga Tjarutja people AU$13.5 million (US$8.5 million) in compensation for displacing them from their land. The Australian government also then spent AU$ 108 million (US$71 million) on decontaminating the Maralinga and Emu sites from 1996 to 2000. The Aboriginal Legal Rights Movement announced in 2010 that it would sue the British Ministry of Defence over diseases and disabilities caused by nuclear tests. So far then the Australian government has paid a total of US$79.83 million in compensation for environmental and health effects of British nuclear tests.

From 1960 until 1965, France conducted 17 nuclear weapons tests at two locations in Algeria. Four of the tests were in the atmosphere and 13 were underground. After Algeria's independence in 1962, the French Defense Department chose alternative test sites in the uninhabited islands of Moruroa and Fangataufa in the South Pacific. However, the atoll of Tureia had some 60 inhabitants and was only 100 km away from Moruroa. France had not signed the PTBT and established a Test Centre at Moruroa in 1966. A total of 193 atmospheric and underground tests were conducted in the region over the next 30 years. From 1975, tests were carried out underground and caused short- and long-term environmental damage. Fracturing of the atoll triggered landslides, tsunamis and earthquakes and radionuclides were released into the environment. Fission products seeped into the biosphere and plutonium leaked away from the lagoon to the ocean and subsequently, the food chain. A Mission to Moruroa by an Australian, New Zealand and Papua New Guinea Mission in 1983 discovered that atmospheric concentrations of plutonium-239 were four times greater than in continental France. Following a number of surveys and worldwide protests, France stopped nuclear tests in 1996 and after much lobbying and campaigning, on 9 January 2009, the French government agreeing to spend over US$80 million to rehabilitate the atoll of

Table 6.5 Health and environmental compensation payments

Japan (1999–2003)	France	Australia	United States
$6.89 billion	$93.5 million	$79.83 million	$9 billion

Source: own elaboration.

Hao in the South Pacific. Long campaigns were also conducted by soldiers and civilians working on the French tests and eventually, on 25 March 2009, the French Ministry of Defence offered ten million Euros (US$13.5 million) as compensation to victims of its test programme. The total costs of compensation for the French nuclear tests so far has been $93.5 million.

Following China's first nuclear test in 1964, they exploded 45 nuclear bombs at the Lop Nor site, which is approximately 265 kilometres southeast of Urumqi in the Xinjiang region in western China. With an area of over 1.6 million square kms, it is the largest Chinese administrative division with a population of 20 million people. There were 23 atmospheric and 22 underground tests and their effects on health, animals and the environment are largely unexplored due to the lack of publicly available data. China claims that, based on over 20 years of surveys, the tests caused no harm to neighbouring countries, nor to the regions of Beijing, Lanzhou or Dunhuang – and anti-nuclear activists say there is no known government programme for compensating victims.

Similarly, there are no known plans to compensate for the nuclear tests conducted by India (six tests between 1974 and 1998 at the Pokhran Test Site) and Pakistan (five devices were exploded in a single test held in 1998 at the Ras Koh Test Site). North Korea has reportedly conducted six nuclear tests at the Punggye-ri Test Site but information about environmental and/or health problems is not forthcoming.

At least $16 billion has so far been paid in compensation and health care to a few of the victims of nuclear weapons and as compensation for some of the environmental damage caused but only after considerable campaigning. This small sum, paid by only two of the nine nuclear weapons states, does not begin to cover the full cost of the damage and suffering caused by the production and testing programmes and the dropping of two bombs on Japan in 1945. The payments have been made to only a fraction of the total number of people affected and there is a considerable amount of environmental damage that is unrepairable and in many cases some of the costs have been incurred by a state other than the one responsible for the damage.

6.6 Conclusion

The world is set to spend at least $125 billion per year on nuclear weapons over the next few years. This is a low estimate of the overall costs that will actually be incurred and does not include sizeable hidden costs to people and the environment. Even so, it is an absurdly large sum of money to spend on weapons that threaten the existence of all life on Earth. Better spent, this money could go a long way to solving many of the problems that the world faces such as poverty, hunger, curable diseases and climate change.

The Nuclear Non-Proliferation Treaty (NPT), the 50th birthday of which will be celebrated in 2020, includes a legal commitment to disarm and to achieve the goal of a nuclear weapon-free world:

> Each of the Parties to the Treaty undertakes to pursue negotiations in good faith on effective measures relating to cessation of the nuclear arms race at an early date and to nuclear disarmament, and on a Treaty on general and complete disarmament under strict and effective international control.
>
> (United Nations, n.d.a.)

While the NPT allows five states to have nuclear weapons, under the proviso that they negotiate them away 'in good faith' a stronger position is taken by the Treaty on the Prohibition of Nuclear Weapons (TPNW), adopted in July 2017 by the UN General assembly with the support of 122 states. The TPNW includes a comprehensive set of prohibitions on participating in any nuclear weapon activities. These include undertakings not to develop, test, produce, acquire, possess, stockpile, use or threaten to use nuclear weapons. The Treaty further prohibits the deployment of nuclear weapons on national territory and the provision of assistance to any State in the conduct of prohibited activities. The treaty was the result of the International Campaign to Abolish Nuclear Weapons (ICAN), launched in 2007, which grew to become a coalition of NGOs in 100 countries and led a group of non-nuclear states to take the initiative in the UN.

The current activities of the nuclear weapon states in maintaining, modernising and developing new nuclear weapons move us in a totally different direction. The risk of the use of nuclear weapons is increasing and the threshold for this is being lowered. The competition between the superpowers is leading to an arms race at a time when arms control has ever bleaker prospects. This results in a destabilisation of the global security situation, which, in turn, is reflected in the costs of nuclear weapons. They occupy an increasing share of the nuclear weapon states' military budgets not only distancing us from the goal of a nuclear weapon – free world but also polarising the nuclear order between those states that see their security as depending on nuclear deterrence and those states that do not.

The costs that we have managed to obtain some details of are not completely transparent and the humanitarian costs are impossible to quantify and totally unrepresentative of the overall damage caused by nuclear weapons use, production and testing. There are many innocent people who have been the victims of the bomb, without any consideration or compensation. Large areas of land near nuclear test sites have been made uninhabitable after nuclear testing, often in states that do not possess nuclear weapons. This applies particularly to islands in the Pacific Ocean, as discussed, for example, by Ruff (2015).

Finally, we would like to conclude that while the nuclear weapon states insist that nuclear deterrence is necessary and the only way to avoid nuclear war, there are other security paradigms, based on collective and common security, which do not imply the need for nuclear deterrence. As an example, over 110 states have joined regional nuclear weapon-free zones and have decided to abolish the option of going nuclear or have even abandoned nuclear weapons programmes. These states recognise the huge costs involved in developing and maintaining a nuclear arsenal and base their security on multilateral cooperative agreements and in building regional trust without the need for threatening a nuclear apocalypse.

Note

1 Kiritimati was used for nine tests by the UK 1957–1958 and then handed over to Australia in 1958. The US was given permission to use the island for more nuclear tests in 1962 – local islanders and British, New Zealand and Fijian military personnel have suffered from exposure to the radiation from these blasts.

Bibliography

Allen, N., Lawler, D. and Sherlock, R. (2016) 'Donald Trump 'Asked Why US Couldn't Use Nuclear Weapons If He Becomes President', *Daily Telegraph*, 3 August. Available at: https://www.telegraph.co.uk/news/2016/08/03/donald-trump-asked-why-us-cant-use-nuclear-weapons-if-he-becomes/ (Accessed: 21 November, 2019).

Alvarez, R. (2018) 'The Cost of Cleaning Up our Nuke Weapons Waste Is Soaring', *Newsweek*, February. Available at: https://www.newsweek.com/cost-cleaning-our-nuke-weapons-waste-soaring-767006 (Accessed: 21 November, 2019).

Atomic Heritage Foundation (2017), 'Survivors of Hiroshima and Nagasaki, 27 July. Available at: https://www.atomicheritage.org/history/survivors-hiroshima-and-nagasaki (Accessed: 21 November, 2019).

Blair, B., and Brown, M.A. (2011) 'Technical Report', Nuclear Weapons Cost Study, Global Zero Campaign, June. Available at: http://fliphtml5.com/bxhp/hxmd/basic (Accessed: 21 November, 2019).

Borger, J. (2017) 'Trump Team Drawing Up Ffresh Plans to Bolster US Nuclear Arsenal', *The Guardian*, 29 October. Available at: https://www.theguardian.com/world/2017/oct/29/trump-us-nuclear-weapons-arsenal (Accessed: 21 November, 2019).

CBO, Congressional Budget Office (2017a) 'Projected Costs of US Nuclear Forces 2017–2026', February 2017. Available at: http://www.lasg.org/budget/CBO_Projected_costs_US_nuclear_forces_2017-2026.pdf (Accessed: 21 November, 2019).

CBO, Congressional Budget Office (2017b) 'Approaches for Managing the Cost of U.S. Nuclear Forces, 2017 to 2046', October. Available at: https://www.cbo.gov/publication/53211 (Accessed: 21 November, 2019).

CBO, Congressional Budget Office (2019) 'The Projected Costs of U.S. Nuclear Forces, 2019 to 2028', January. Available at: https://www.cbo.gov/system/files?file=2019-01/54914-NuclearForces.pdf (Accessed: 21 November, 2019).

Cirincione, J. (2005) 'Lessons Lost', *Bulletin of the Atomic Scientists*, November/December 2005, p. 47.

CND, Campaign for Nuclear Disarmament (2016) 'The Costs of Replacing Trident'. Available at: https://cnduk.org/wp-content/uploads/2018/02/Costs-2016-web.pdf (Accessed: 21 November, 2019).

Cramer, B. (2009) *Nuclear Weapons: At What Cost?* IPB Publication, July.

Cronberg, T. (2010) 'Nuclear-Free Security. Refocusing Nuclear Disarmament and the Review of the Nuclear Non-Proliferation Treaty', *Finnish Institute of International Affairs*, Report 21.

CTBTO, Comprehensive Test Ban Treaty Organisation (n.d.) 'The Manhattan Project'. Available at: https://www.ctbto.org/nuclear-testing/ (Accessed: 21 November, 2019).

Gerson, J. (2007) *Empire and the Bomb: How the United States Uses Nuclear Weapons to Dominate the World*, London: Pluto Press and University of Michigan Press.

Harrington de Santana, A. (2009) 'Nuclear Weapons as the Currency of Power – Deconstructing the Fetishism of Force', *Nonproliferation Review*, 16:3, 325–345.

Hiroshima for Global Peace (2003), *Summary of Relief Measures for Atomic Bomb Survivors*, Atomic Bomb Survivors Relief Department of the Social Affairs Bureau in the City of Hiroshima. Available at: http://www.city.hiroshima.lg.jp/shimin/heiwa/relief.pdf (Accessed: 21 November 2019).

HMG, Her Majesty's Government (2010a) 'Securing Britain in an Age of Uncertainty: The Strategic Defence and Security Review' para. 3.11. Available at https://webarchive.nationalarchives.gov.uk/20121018082048/http://www.direct.gov.uk/prod_consum_dg/groups/dg_digitalassets/@dg/@en/documents/digitalasset/dg_191634.pdf (Accessed: 21 November, 2019).

HMG, Her Majesty's Government (2010b) 'Treaty between the United Kingdom of Great Britain and Northern Ireland and the French Republic Relating to Joint Radiographic/Hydrodynamics Facilities', 2 November. Available at: https://assets.publishing.service.gov.uk/government/uploads/system/uploads/attachment_data/file/228571/7975.pdf (Accessed: 21 November, 2019).

HMG, Her Majesty's Government (2015) 'National Security Strategy and Strategic Defence and Security Review 2015'. Available at: https://www.gov.uk/government/publications/national-security-strategy-and-strategic-defence-and-security-review-2015 (Accessed: 21 November, 2019).

House of Commons Library (2019) 'The Cost of the UK's Strategic Nuclear Deterrent', January 22. Available at: https://researchbriefings.parliament.uk/ResearchBriefing/Summary/CBP-8166 (Accessed: 21 November, 2019).

Japan News (2019), '*World Free of Nuclear Weapons Urged at Hiroshima Ceremony*', The *Japan News, 6 August*. Available at. https://the-japan-news.com/news/article/0005922619 (Accessed: 21 November, 2019).

Kaplan, F. (2001) 'JFK's First-Strike Plan', *The Atlantic*, October 2001. Available at: https://www.theatlantic.com/magazine/archive/2001/10/jfks-first-strike-plan/376432/ (Accessed: 21 November, 2019).

Kile, S. and Kristensen, H.M. (2017) 'French Nuclear Forces' *SIPRI Yearbook*. Available at https://www.sipri.org/sites/default/files/SIPRIYB18c06.pdf (Accessed: 21 November, 2019).

Kristensen, H.M. (2006) *Britain's Next Nuclear Era, Federation of American Scientists,* 7 December. Available at: https://fas.org/blogs/security/2006/12/britains_next_nuclear_era/ (Accessed: 21 November, 2019).

Kristensen, H.M. and Korda, M. (2019a) *Status of World Nuclear Forces,* Federation of American Scientists, May. Available at: https://fas.org/issues/nuclear-weapons/status-world-nuclear-forces/ (Accessed: 21 November, 2019).

Kristensen, H.M. and Korda, M. (2019b) 'United States Nuclear Forces, 2019', *Bulletin of the Atomic Scientists,* 75:3, 122–134. Available at: https://doi.org/10.1080/00963402.2019.1606503 (Accessed: 21 November, 2019).

Kristensen, H.M. and Korda, M. (2019c) 'French Nuclear Forces, 2019', *Bulletin of the Atomic Scientists,* 75:1, 51–55. Available at: https://www.tandfonline.com/doi/full/10.1080/00963402.2019.1556003 (Accessed: 21 November, 2019).

Norris, R.S. and Kristensen, H.M. (2013) 'The British Nuclear Stockpile, 1953–2013', *Bulletin of the Atomic Scientists,* 69:4, 69–75. Available at: https://journals.sagepub.com/doi/pdf/10.1177/0096340213493260 (Accessed: 21 November, 2019).

Parly, F. (2017) 'Speech by Florence Parly, Minister of the Armed Forces, Visit to the Mureaux factory: Ariane Group, Mureaux', 14 December. Available at: https://www.defense.gouv.fr/actualites/communaute-defense/discours-de-florence-parly-ministre-des-armees-prononce-a-l-usine-des-mureaux-arianegroup-le-14-decembre-2017 (Accessed: 21 November, 2019).

Parly, F. (2018) 'Speech by Florence Parly, Minister of Defence -60 years of DAM', French Ministry of the Armed Forces, Paris, 21 November. Available at: https://www.defense.gouv.fr/salle-de-presse/discours/discours-de-florence-parly/discours-de-florence-parly-ministre-des-armees-60-ans-de-la-dam (Accessed: 21 November, 2019).

Reif, K. (2017) *CBO: Nuclear Arsenal to Cost $1.2 Trillion,* Arms Control Association, December. Available at: https://www.armscontrol.org/act/2017-12/news/cbo-nuclear-arsenal-cost-12-trillion (Accessed: 21 November, 2019).

Ruff, T.A. (2015) 'The Humanitarian Impact and Implications of Nuclear Test Explosions in the Pacific Region', *International Review of the Red Cross,* 97: 899, 775–813. Available at: https://www.icrc.org/en/international-review/article/humanitarian-impact-and-implications-nuclear-test-explosions-pacific (Accessed: 21 November, 2019).

Schell, J. (2007) *The Seventh Decade: The New Shape of Nuclear Danger (American Empire Project),* New York: Metropolitan Books.

Schwartz, S. (1998) *Atomic Audit: The Costs and Consequences of U.S. Nuclear Weapons since 1940,* Brookings Institution Press. Available at: https://www.brookings.edu/book/atomic-audit/ (Accessed: 21 November, 2019).

Schwartz, S. (2008) *The Costs of U.S. Nuclear Weapons,* Nuclear Files, October. Available at: http://www.nuclearfiles.org/menu/key-issues/nuclear-weapons/issues/policy/us-nuclear-policy/costs2.htm#fn3 (Accessed: 21 November, 2019).

SIPRI, Stockholm International Peace Research Institute (2019), *World Nuclear Forces,* Year Book. Available at: https://www.sipri.org/yearbook/2019/06 (Accessed: 21 November, 2019).

Taureck, R. (2006) 'Securitization Theory and Securitization Studies,' *Journal of International Relations Dev* 9, 53–61.

Taylor, T. (2018) 'Nevada Test Site Downwinders,' Atomic Heritage Foundation, https://www.atomicheritage.org/history/nevada-test-site-downwinders, (Accessed: 21 May, 2020).

United Nations (n.d.a.) Treaty on the Non-Proliferation of Nuclear Weapons (NPT). Text of the Treaty, https://www.un.org/disarmament/wmd/nuclear/npt/text/ (Accessed: 30 April, 2020).

UNSCEAR (2000) Sources and effects of ionizing radiation. United Nations Scientific Committee on the Effects of Atomic Radiation UNSCEAR 2000 Report to the General Assembly, with Scientific Annexes, United Nations, New York.

Zala, B. (2019) 'How the next nuclear arms race will be different from the last one', Bulletin of the Atomic Scientists, vol. 75, no. 1, pp. 36–43.

7 Military spending and climate change

Chloé Meulewaeter and Pere Brunet

7.1 Introduction

The scientific community agrees that climate change will have catastrophic consequences during the next decades if it is not reversed, while humanity is pushing Earth's ecosystems beyond its capacities. We are fast approaching many of the limits of what the biosphere can tolerate without substantial and irreversible harm (Ripple, Wolf, et al., 2017).

In this chapter we aim to show the connections between climate change, global power and military spending. In Section 7.2, we briefly present the warnings of scientists on climate change. In Section 7.3, we discuss the concept of the Global Triangle of Power, which includes transnational corporations (most of them extractive), the military-industrial complex and global financial entities. In Section 7.4, we proceed to relate climate change to the Global Triangle of Power. In Section 7.5, we show how military spending, as the first stage of the military-economic cycle, involves huge environmental impacts and thus might be a key factor in global warming. Finally, we conclude with the main findings of our investigation, and we present some recommendations aimed at mitigating the effects of climate change, mainly based on reducing military spending and the size of the Global Triangle of Power.

7.2 Climate change: a scientific view

Twenty-seven years ago, in November 1992, around 1,700 scientists from around the world, including the majority of Nobel laureates in life sciences at that time (Abragam, Anatole, Aguirre, Carlos, et al., 1997), warned mankind. They said that human activities cause damage that is often irreversible to the environment and to critical resources, and that many of our current practices place the future we want for human society and the plant and animal biosphere in serious jeopardy, so that it can end up threatening the entire living world. They explained that it was very urgent to make fundamental changes in order to avoid the collision that we were preparing. They stated that developed nations are the largest polluters in the world today, and that:

> Success in this global endeavour will require a great reduction in violence and war. Resources now devoted to the preparation and conduct of war, amounting to over $1 trillion annually, will be badly needed in the new tasks and should be diverted to the new challenges.
>
> (Abragam, Aguirre, et al., 1997)

The scientific journal Bioscience published in 2018 an article signed by 15,372 scientists from 184 countries (Ripple, Wolf, et al., 2017). With the strength of these 15 thousand signatures, the article discusses the alarming trends in the indicators they have been studying, and notes that humans have ignored the first scientists' warning (Abragam, Aguirre, et al., 1997). The authors give a second warning to humanity, saying that with our disproportionate consumption and with our rapid population growth, we are not sustainable, and we are endangering our future. They affirm that there are a lot of efforts generated by "organizations that come from the people", in order to overcome the current stubborn opposition to changes and to force political leaders "to do what needs to be done", according to scientific evidence.

According to Steffen, Rockström, et al. (2018), self-reinforcing feedbacks can push the earth's system towards a planetary threshold that, if crossed, could prevent stabilization of the climate. Crossing the threshold would lead to a much higher global average temperature than any interglacial period in the past 1.2 million years, and also to serious disruptions to ecosystems, society and economies.

7.3 The Global Triangle of Power

Neoliberalism has created the conditions under which our governments are co-opted by corporations, being therefore wedded to short-term strategies of profit-seeking that cannot deliver a fair, efficient, or peaceful response to the devastating impacts of climate change (Buxton and Hayes, 2015). In fact, during the 20th century, large multinational corporations have moved from being controlled by state governments to themselves controlling these national states. As Buxton and Hayes (2015) argue

> It is the state that feeds the military-industrial complex, and the state that acts as the prime backer of the corporate takeover of land, water, food and energy, removing regulations and opening up markets to them, negotiating trade deals on their behalf, and creating what some scholars call an international legal "architecture of impunity" for corporations, which has escalated human rights abuses and corporate crimes worldwide. This is because corporations have in many ways captured states;

populating their ministries with staff, designing their policies, lobbying against regulation, and threatening boycott and withdrawal if any state dares to challenge them.

(Buxton and Hayes, 2015)

A rigorous analysis of the global network of economic control has been carried out by Vitali, Glattfelder, et al. (2011). They discovered that there is a strongly connected nucleus of multinational corporations (mainly financial institutions) that exercise a powerful control over a host of other companies in all countries. Previous studies were basically country-based, and therefore could not analyse the global power of current transnational corporations.

Vitali, Glattfelder, et al. (2011) start from a genuine concept of economic and financial control. Their definition states that the corporations with a very high level of control are those who can potentially impose their decisions on many economically strong companies. The authors start from the 30 million companies and economic actors in the Orbis 2007 database, and from a list of 43,060 transnational corporations published by OECD. Their study is based on the construction and analysis of a mathematical relationship graph among companies. The authors analyse the graph of companies either controlled by a transnational corporation or controlling a transnational corporation. This results in a graph with 600,508 nodes (companies) and 1,006,987 control arches. The graph shows a large connected component with 463,006 economic actors and 889,601 relationships. The main finding of Vitali and her colleagues (Vitali, Glattfelder, et al., 2011) is the fact that a group of 737 shareholders accumulates control of 80% of all transnational corporations in the world. That is, 0.61% of transnational corporations' shareholders control 80% of all major world corporations.

Moreover, Vitali and her colleagues present, as a partial result, the top 50 main actors that control the entire network of companies worldwide. They show that these 50 shareholders (many of them are financial entities) already control 39.78% of all transnational corporations (the top 737 having effective control of the 80% of all transnational corporations). The interest of this ranking is not only that it reveals the list of the most powerful corporations, but also that it shows that many of these main actors belong to a core that forms an extremely dense and linked network of control. They do not perform business in isolation; on the contrary, they are united. The list of these 50 shareholders includes large extractive corporations, banks and financial multinational corporations (Vitali, Glattfelder, et al., 2011).

As shown in Figure 7.1, the Global Triangle of Power represents the linkage between the military-industrial complex, global financial entities and extractive transnational corporations. It is detailed as follows:

-   Extractive corporations and the military-industrial complex: extractive transnational corporations demand military protection, to secure the extraction and transport of all resources (Buxton and Hayes, 2015).

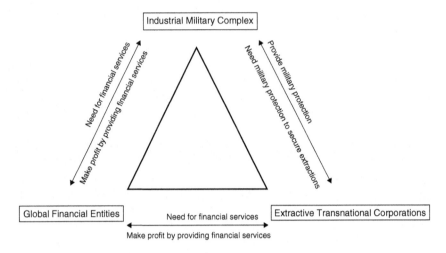

Figure 7.1 The Global Triangle of Power.
Source: own elaboration.

- Extractive transnational corporations and global financial entities: as any other company, extractive transnational corporations need financial services.
- The military-industrial complex and extractive transnational corporations: ensuring the secure operation of extractive transnational corporations is an increasingly important mission of the military (Buxton and Hayes, 2015).
- The military-industrial complex and global financial entities: the military needs financial services in order to ensure the proper functioning of the process of militarization, as the Armed Banking campaign shows.[1]
- Global financial entities and extractive transnational corporations: financial institutions make business from loans to extractive transnational corporations. Moreover, a small number of global financial entities is now controlling transnational corporations (Vitali, Glattfelder, et al., 2011).
- Global financial entities and the military-industrial complex: financial institutions make profit from loans to military industries, by financing both production and arms trade.[1] This is a profitable business because arms companies are supported by governments.

We observe that the Global Triangle of Power is a tightly connected network of individuals and organizations that is autonomous, and represents undemocratic institutions (Buxton and Hayes, 2015). In addition, the Global Triangle of Power is characterized by the interdependence of its components: the survival of each of them is related to the other two. As Dwight D. Eisenhower stated in his 1961 speech:

> In the councils of government, we must guard against the acquisition of unwarranted influence, whether sought or unsought, by the military industrial complex. The potential for the disastrous rise of misplaced power exists and will persist.
>
> (Eisenhower, 1961: Item IV)

The Global Triangle of Power is self-driving, expanding and growing year after year because of the converging interests of its three components. It profits from the advantage of being global in a world of many different national states that often turn to militarized solutions when trying to sustain exploitative, extractive projects (War Resisters International, 2019). As a result, one of its outputs is climate change, as we will discuss next.

7.4 Climate change: a consequence of the Global Triangle of Power

Large extractive corporations are often responsible for exploiting the resources of the Global South countries, leading to an increase in the rate of global warming. Also, these corporations, as we explain above, require militarized protection and therefore have to lobby governments to increase military spending, to ensure an effective level of military force (Buxton and Hayes, 2015). Moreover, an analysis of the Global Triangle of Power and its growing dynamics leads to several main conclusions:

- The Global Triangle of Power successfully uses lobbying to ensure the private interests of its components, also implementing economic, military and financial control over most corporations and states. The results of lobbying actions come in the form of influence over national governments, and in receiving substantial public funds. Lobbying actions by extractive corporations, the military-industrial complex and global financial entities have been extensively documented.
- Predatory business by extractive transnational corporations requires violence, and the need for violence demands militarized security (Buxton and Hayes, 2015).
- The military-industrial complex in the Global North produces and exports most of the global weapons, in a non-stop arms trade business.
- A fundamental goal of the institutions in the Global Triangle of Power is to increase their revenues and benefits while having control over the maximum number of organizations (Vitali, Glattfelder, et al., 2011).
- The Global Triangle of Power works to defend the interests of a minority of people in the Global North, at the expense of devouring the planet's resources, mainly in countries of the Global South (Buxton and Hayes, 2015).

- Militarized security might be a key factor in global warming, and military operations involve huge environmental impacts (Meulewaeter, 2017).
- Institutions of the Global Triangle of Power can only increase their profits by exploiting more and more of the planet's energy and resources, which leads to global warming. By trying to maintain the living standards and security level of the North's citizens, institutions in the Global Triangle of Power warm the planet (Buxton, 2018), boosting climate change.

Figure 7.2 illustrates the relationship between climate change and the Global Triangle of Power through the evolution of five different indicators: (1) the loss of global equality (dotted) is measured as the number of billionaires it takes to equal the wealth of the bottom 50% of the global population (Inequality.org, 2019); (2) the arms trade (striped) is measured by the trend in international transfers of major weapons (SIPRI, 2019b); (3) the number of EU border walls (continuous) (Ruiz Benedicto and Brunet, 2018); (4) data of the surface area (billion Ha, in grey) and (5) the average planet temperature (in dots and stripes) (Ripple, Wolf, et al., 2017).

Figure 7.2 shows increasing arms trade, with global wealth and power becoming more and more concentrated, and with increasing inequalities. We observe, on the other hand, accelerated global warming and constant decrease in forest surface area. Regarding climate change and military power, there is a clear inverse correlation between the loss of global equality and planet warming and a correlation between warming and arms trade since 2014 (arms trade shows an increasing trend, with an exceptional peak in 2011).

Moreover, Figure 7.1 illustrates the geographical distribution of the Global Triangle of Power and of the related climate threats. It shows the ten main arms exporters in 2018, the ten countries hosting the 45 top global agents of corporate control in 2011, the top ten countries having maximum climate risk in 2014, the 20 countries with a high or medium rate of armed conflicts in 2018, and the top ten countries with proven oil reserves in 2019.

Figure 7.3 shows that the Global Triangle of Power is located in the Global North, and that the associated climate threats are concentrated in the Global South. Indeed, the line separates two main regions. Above, in the Global North, are the ten countries that export the most (the USA, Russia, France, Germany, China, the UK, Spain, Israel, Italy and the Netherlands); the ten countries controlling a significant amount of all transnational corporations (the USA, the UK, France, Japan, Switzerland, the Netherlands, Germany, China, Canada and Italy) (see Annex 3). Below the line, in the Global South, are the countries most threatened by climate change: Bangladesh, Guinea-Bissau, Sierra Leone, Haiti, South Sudan, Nigeria, Democratic Republic of Congo, Cambodia, Philippines and Ethiopia. It is in this part of the world that countries in situations of armed conflict are also found, with the exception of Turkey and Ukraine (countries

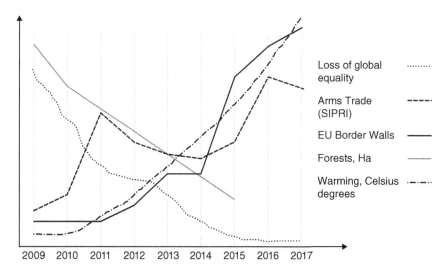

Year	Inequality (1)	Arms Trade (2)	EU Border walls (3)	Deforestation (4)	Warming (5)
2009	380	24,234	2	4016	0.98
2010	211	25,691	2	4013	0.98
2011	135	30,006	2	4010	0.99
2012	135	28,289	3	4007	1.02
2013	83	26,954	5	4003	1.08
2014	62	26,780	5	4000	1.14
2015	55	28,522	12	3997	1.20
2016	61	32,262	14	No data	1.26
2017	42	31,106	15	No data	1.32

Figure 7.2 Evolution of the loss of global equality, global arms trade, number of EU
border walls, forests in the planet and average Earth temperature, years
2009–2016.

Source: Inequality.org (2019); SIPRI (2019); Ruiz Benedicto and Brunet (2018); Ripple,
Wolf, et al. (2017).[2]

are listed in Annex 3). Northern oil reserves are mainly located in Canada
(169.7 million barrels) but also in Russia (80 million barrels) and the USA
(39.2 million barrels). But oil reserves in the seven main countries located in
the South (Venezuela, Saudi Arabia, Iran, Iraq, Kuwait, the UAE, Libya) is
1115.9 million barrels. Thus 79.4% of the present oil reserves of the top ten
countries lie in the South.

As already discussed, the Global Triangle of Power is self-driving. It ex-
pands and grows year after year because of the converging interests of its
network of interests and power (its size and rate of growth can be measured
by the total amount of revenues). Climate change is therefore an inevitable
by-product of "business as usual" in the Global Triangle of Power.

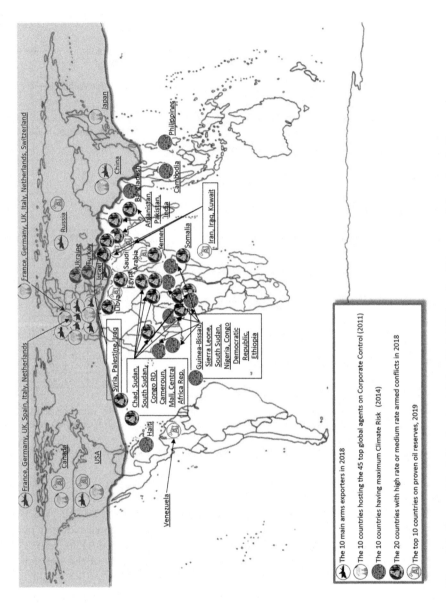

The 10 main arms exporters in 2018

The 10 countries hosting the 45 top global agents on Corporate Control (2011)

The 10 countries having maximum Climate Risk   (2014)

The 20 countries with high rate or medium rate armed conflicts in 2018

The top 10 countries on proven oil reserves, 2019

Figure 7.3 Geographical distribution of the Global Triangle of Power and the related climate threats.
Source: own elaboration[3] some errors in the box above, see previous para.

Moreover, climate change increases the risk of violent conflict, as Parkinson states (2018). The author argues that lack of finance is often put forward as an excuse for unambitious action on climate change, while at the same time military budgets are being expanded. Instead, tackling climate change would make a major contribution to improving security. Also, the presumption that climate change represents a security issue – thus involving the military apparatus – might be seen the other way around: militarized security might be a key factor in global warming (Meulewaeter, 2017). Indeed, in the past few decades, not only have the carbon emissions increased, but also global military spending. As the first stage of the military-economic cycle, military expenditure is producing huge environmental impacts, as shown in the next section.

7.5 On the link between military spending and climate change

Military spending used to be considered as a guarantee of security, and therefore as an investment in peace. Contrary to this common presumption, public defence budget – as the first step of the military-economic cycle – might be a factor of insecurity and a driver of the use of armed force.

One effect of military expenditure is its impact on environment. There are at least three reasons that illuminate the link between the military and the global climate change:

-   First, expensive weapons systems – such as fighter jets, battleships, fighting vehicles, destroyers and tanks – are extremely energy-inefficient, and huge oil consumers. In fact, it has been proved that worldwide military activity is the largest institutional emitter of greenhouse gases (Schwartz, Blakeley, et al., 2012; Crawford, 2019).
-   Second, the ecological effects of war and military activity in general include wetland degradation, water pollution, deforestation and the contamination of agricultural land (Archer, 2013).
-   Third, military expenditure means fewer resources for environmental and social policies, due to the opportunity cost of less money available to mitigate and adapt to climate change.

Those three points are found at different stages of the military-economic cycle (Calvo Rufanges, 2015), as we can see in Figure 7.4. The military-economic cycle illustrates the process of militarization and arms build-up of a society. It states that the responsibility for the facility with which armed violence is used to tackle security threats lies in the inertia of the military-economic cycle, which is based on the annual approval of the defence spending of a country.

As a theoretical framework, the economic military cycle provides an understanding of how climate change is inherent in the process of militarization of a society. Indeed, the increase of military spending supposes more military R&D, more production of extremely energy-inefficient and huge

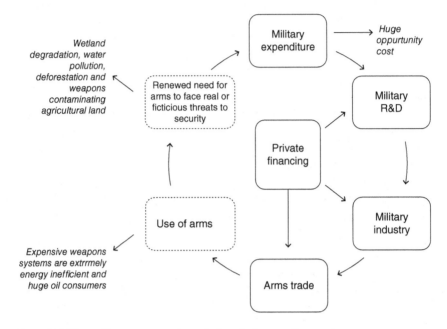

Figure 7.4 The military-economic cycle in relation to climate change.
Source: own elaboration.

oil-consuming weapons, more arms trade, and ultimately the use of those weapons in armed conflicts, provoking wetland degradation, water pollution, deforestation and agricultural land contamination. The consequent repeated need for arms, intended for tackling real or fictitious threats to security, is in fact a direct consequence of the self-amplification of the Global Triangle of Power: a constant amplification and expansion that results in conflicts, resource depredation, warming, iniquities and poverty. Moreover, the annual approval of public defence budgets creates a huge opportunity cost, limiting the possibility to finance policies to mitigate climate change and other social policies, all related to human security and well-being.

Over the past decades, not only carbon emissions have drastically increased, so has military expenditure. SIPRI (2019) estimates that global military spending reached US$1014 billion in 1998 and rose to US$1774 billion in 2018 (2017 constant prices, excluding Iraq), which means almost 60% increase in 20 years. In current prices, global military spending was $1816 billion and accounted for 2.1% of global gross domestic product. This figure is the highest since the end of the Cold War and has increased significantly after five years of stagnation. That is why the role of the carbon emissions of the military on global warming must be called into consideration when it is known that the US army is the largest consumer of oil in the USA and the largest industrial consumer of oil in the world (Schwartz, Blakeley, et al., 2012, Crawford, 2019). Maintaining the biggest war machine in the world, prepared to go to war, requires a huge amount of energy consumption and fuel. Incidentally, back to 1992, the CO_2 emissions by the military were explicitly excluded from the Kyoto Protocol (Graham-Leigh, 2019), so the military, on the one hand, could keep business as usual, and on the other hand, media and social awareness on environmental issues would not jeopardize war. Later, the exclusion was removed in the 2015 Paris agreement, but was still not mandatory.

A recent investigation based on 158 countries for the period 1960–2015 has found a positive relationship between the military – in particular military expenditure – and CO_2 emissions (Meulewaeter, 2017). Several issues could be highlighted from the estimations. First, military expenditure influences CO_2 emissions. The greater the military expenditure, the higher the CO_2 emissions. Second, the influence of military expenditure on CO_2 emissions is independent of the environmental Kuznets curve, meaning that military expenditure has an influence that goes beyond its productive role. That is, military expenditure, by itself, is a determinant of CO_2 emissions and thus is responsible for worsening climate change. For example, according to the estimations, the 3.91% increase in world military spending per capita between 2017 and 2018 ($230 per capita in 2017, $239 per capita in 2018) led to 2.7 kilos increase in CO_2 emissions per capita worldwide. To get an idea of the magnitude of this figure we can compare it to the CO_2 emissions of the US military. Crawford (2019) estimated the CO_2 emissions of the Department of Defense of the USA in 2017 at 59 millions of metric tons. This represents approximately 180 kilos per capita in the USA and 7.8 kilos of CO_2 emissions per capita worldwide.

These findings warn against the current tendency to consider global warming as a security issue, within the framework of the militarized security paradigm that characterizes our society. Nevertheless, as scientists agree (see Mach, Kraan, et al., 2019, for an analysis published in *Nature* by a group of experts), climate change does represent a growing risk factor for armed conflict. As they state:

> Climate variability and change are estimated to have substantially increased risk across 5% of conflicts to date (mean estimated by experts). By contrast, an approximately 2°C increase in the global mean temperature above preindustrial levels is estimated to substantially increase conflict risk with 13% probability, rising to 26% probability under an approximately 4°C warming scenario.
>
> (Mach, Kraan, et al., 2019: 194)

Global warming, seen as a "threat multiplier" that influences other existing threats, can in no way legitimize the increased use of the military for security reasons, nor justify such alarming trends in global military expenditure. The military as a whole is a key determinant of global warming. There is a possibility of reallocation of resources from military expenditure to climate change, fostering climate resilience and encouraging low greenhouse gas emissions development. Since climate change is one of the main threats to security, there is an urgent need to redefine security from military roles to human security in order to properly reallocate military budgets into environment-related expenditures that may be more efficient and consistent with efforts to tackle the climate emergency.

7.6 Conclusions

As mentioned in Steffen, Rockström, et al. (2018), the planet warming that we are fostering is about to launch several mechanisms that can accelerate it in an unstoppable way: the loss of permafrost, the increase in bacterial respiration in the oceans, the reduction of ice in the polar zones and many other phenomena that are going to be activated in cascade. However, scientists agree that there is still time to drive the planet towards a quasi-stable state.

In this chapter, we state that climate change is an inevitable by-product of "business as usual" of the Global Triangle of Power. The extractive transnational corporations, the military-industrial complex and the global financial entities that are part of it get significant benefits independently of democratic institutions. This triangle is self-driving, expanding and growing year after year because of the converging interests of its three components. It profits from the advantage of being global in a world of many different states that lack global regulations and worldwide democratic institutions. From this concept, we present two main findings.

First, we have observed that all agents of the Global Triangle of Power are located in the Global North, while the countries most threatened by climate change are in the Global South, where the largest oil reserves and the highest number of armed conflicts are located. Climate change affecting the South is an unavoidable by-product of "business as usual" in the Global Triangle of Power. Second, we have shown that military spending is one of the driving forces of the Global Triangle of Power and that military activities have an impact on climate change. As the largest global user of oil, and the main producer of greenhouse gases around the world, the military is a determinant of global warming. As our empirical analysis demonstrates, the incidence of military spending on CO_2 emissions is independent of the environmental Kuznets curve, meaning that the military is a determinant of global warming by itself.

In this context, we consider that a global reduction of military spending, together with a redirection of these funds to cover human needs and to enhance global human security, would be a tool to reduce global warming and to mitigate the effects of climate change.

Notes

1 More information about Armed Banking campaign can be found in its website www.bancaarmada.org.
2 (1) Number of billionaires it takes to equal the wealth of the bottom 50% of the global population. Data from: https://inequality.org/facts/global-inequality/ (2) SIPRI: Trend in international transfers of major weapons (figures in SIPRI

Trend Indicator Values, TIVs, expressed in millions): http://armstrade.sipri.org/armstrade/page/trade_values.php (3) Number of EU border walls to stop persons wishing to come to Europe. From the "Building Walls Report: European Union Walls that stop persons with militarized security measures": http://www.centredelas.org/images/INFORMES_i_altres_PDF/informe35_Building Walls_ENG.pdf (4) Forests surface area (Million Ha): from William J. Ripple, Christopher Wolf, Thomas M. Newsome, Mauro Galetti, Mohammed Alamgir, Eileen Crist, Mahmoud I. Mahmoud, William F. Laurance and 15,364 scientist signatories from 184 countries (2017): "World Scientists' Warning to Humanity: A Second Notice", Bioscience Volume 67, Issue 12, December 2017, Pages 1026–1028: https://academic.oup.com/bioscience/article/67/12/1026/4605229 Data from the FAO 2015 Report on Global Forest Resources Assessment 2015: How are the world's forests changing?: http://www.fao.org/3/a-i4793e.pdf (5) Planet warming (average planet temperature): from William J. Ripple, Christopher Wolf, Thomas M. Newsome, Mauro Galetti, Mohammed Alamgir, Eileen Crist, Mahmoud I. Mahmoud, William F. Laurance and 15,364 scientist signatories from 184 countries (2017): "World Scientists' Warning to Humanity: A Second Notice", Bioscience Volume 67, Issue 12, December 2017, Pages 1026–1028: https://academic.oup.com/bioscience/article/67/12/1026/4605229 Data (land annual mean temperature with respect to 1951-1980, using Lowess-5 smoothing) available from NASA's Goddard's Institute for Space Studies: https://data.giss.nasa.gov/gistemp/ - available at: https://data.giss.nasa.gov/gistemp/graphs_v4/graph_data/Temperature_Anomalies_over_Land_and_over_Ocean/graph.txt.

3   The ten main arms exporters in 2018 (the USA, Russia, France, Germany, China, the UK, Spain, Israel, Italy and the Netherlands): SIPRI, "Trends in International Arms Transfers 2018", Pieter D. Wezeman et al.: https://www.sipri.org/sites/default/files/2019-03/fs_1903_at_2018.pdf

The ten countries hosting the 45 top global agents of corporate control (2011). These agents are corporations from the financial sector. This list of 45 includes the top ones when ranked by network control of other transnational corporations. Together, they concentrate 36.58% of the world's corporate control. Network control is defined according to the TM model (full control over a company is assigned to the actor holding a number of shares higher than a predefined threshold (50% in our case), while the other holders are assigned zero control). This list of ten countries includes the USA (20 agents), the UK (eight agents), France (five agents), Japan (four agents), Switzerland (two agents), the Netherlands (two agents), and Germany, China, Canada and Italy (one agent each). From Vitali (2011) data appendix: https://doi.org/10.1371/journal.pone.0025995.s001

The top ten countries having maximum climate risk, 2014 (Bangladesh, Guinea-Bissau, Sierra Leone, Haiti, South Sudan, Nigeria, Congo Democratic Republic, Cambodia, Philippines, Ethiopia): World Climate Change Vulnerability Index 2014: https://reliefweb.int/map/world/world-climate-change-vulnerability-index-2014

The 20 countries with high or medium rate armed conflicts in 2018 (Libya, Mali, Chad, Somalia, South Sudan, Iraq, Syria, Yemen, Afghanistan, Congo Democratic Republic, Cameroon, Central African Republic, Sudan, Philippines, India, Pakistan, Egypt, Palestine, Turkey and Ukraine). Report 2018 of the Escola de Cultura de Pau on Conflicts, Human Rights and Peace Culture. Autonomous University of Barcelona (in Spanish): https://escolapau.uab.cat/img/programas/alerta/alerta/19/alerta19e.pdf

The top ten countries with proven oil reserves (Venezuela, Saudi Arabia, Canada, Iran, Iraq, Kuwait, the UAE, Russia, Libya and the USA). From: Oil reserves by country. World Atlas, The World's Largest Oil Reserves By Country (January 8, 2019): https://www.worldatlas.com/articles/the-world-s-largest-oil-reserves-by-country.html

Bibliography

Abragam, Anatole, Aguirre, Carlos, et al. (1997), *World scientists warning to humanity*. Union of Concerned Scientists. Available at: https://www.ucsusa.org/sites/default/files/attach/2017/11/World%20Scientists%27%20Warning%20to%20Humanity%201992.pdf.

Archer, Colin (2013), Military spending and the UN's development agenda. In: *Peace Review: A Journal of Social Justice*, 25, 24–32.

Buxton, Nick (2018), Climate change, capitalism and the military. The Ecologist. Available at: https://theecologist.org/2018/nov/15/climate-change-capitalism-and-military, Access date: 10 June 2019.

Buxton, Nick and Hayes, Ben (2015), *The secure and the dispossessed: How the military and corporations are shaping a climate-changed world*. London: Pluto Press.

Calvo Rufanges, Jordi (2015), El ciclo económico militar. In: Calvo Rufanges, Jordi and Pozo Marín, Alejandro (coords.) *Diccionario de la Guerra la paz y el desarme*. Barcelona: Icaria, p. 81–84.

Calvo Rufanges, Jordi, Ruiz Benedicto, Ainhoa et al. (2017), *European arms that foster armed conflicts, that cause refugees to flee*. Barcelona: Centre Delàs d'Estudis per la Pau.

Crawford, Neta C. (2019), *Pentagon fuel use, climate change, and the costs of war*. Watson Institute, Brown University. Available at: https://watson.brown.edu/costsofwar/files/cow/imce/papers/2019/Pentagon%20Fuel%20Use, %20Climate%20Change %20and%20the%20Costs%20of%20War%20Final.pdf Access date: 10 June 2019.

Eisenhower, Dwight D. (1961), *The military-industrial complex speech*. Available at: http://avalon.law.yale.edu/20th_century/eisenhower001.asp Access date: 10 June 2019.

Fleurant, Aude, Kuimova, Alexandra, et al. (2018), The SIPRI Top 100 arms-producing and military services companies, 2017. SIPRI. Available at: https://www.sipri.org/publications/2018/sipri-fact-sheets/sipri-top-100-arms-producing-and-military-services-companies-2017 Access date: 16 July 2019.

Graham-Leigh (2019), Why stopping wars is essential for stopping climate change? *Stop the War Coalition*. Available at: http://www.stopwar.org.uk/index.php/news-comment/3308-why-stopping-wars-is-essential-for-stopping-climate-change Access date: 10 July 2019.

Hickel, Jason (2016), Time for degrowth: To save the planet, we must shrink the economy. *The Conversation*. Available at: http://theconversation.com/time-for -degrowth-to-save-the-planet-we-must-shrink-the-economy-64195 Access date: 10 June 2019.

Inequality.org (2019), *Global inequality*. Available at: https://inequality.org/facts/global-inequality/ Access date: 10 June 2019.

Mach, Katharine J., Kraan, Caroline M., et al. (2019), Climate as a risk factor for armed conflict. In: *Nature*, 571, 193–197.

Mayor Zaragoza, Federico. (2011), The crime of silence: The time has come, it's time for action. Fundación Cultura de Paz. Available at: http://www.fund -culturadepaz.org/doc/The_Crime_of_Silence_FM.pdf

Meulewaeter, Chloé (2017), Peace, war and ecology: Is the military an issue for climate change? In: György Pataki (chair), *12th Conference of the European Society for Ecological Economics*, Budapest, Hungary. Available at: http://esee2017budapest .org/wp-content/uploads/2016/06/ESEE-2017-Proceedings-1.pdf Access date: 20 June 2019.

NASA (2015), NASA releases detailed global climate change projections. Available at: https://www.nasa.gov/press-release/nasa-releases-detailed-global-climate-change-projections Access date: 10 June 2019.

Parkinson, Stuart (2018), Military spending hits record levels, while climate finance falls short. In: *Scientists for Global Responsability*. Available at: http://www.sgr.org.uk/resources/military-spending-hits-record-levels-while-climate-finance-falls-short Access date: 10 June 2019.

Ripple, William J., Wolf, Christopher, et al. (2017), World scientists' warning to humanity: A second notice. In: *Bioscience*, 67, 12, 1026–1028.

Ruiz Benedicto, Ainhoa, Brunet, Pere (2018), *Building walls: Fear and securitization in the European Union*. Barcelona, Centre Delàs d'Estudis per la Pau.

Schwartz, Moshe, Blakeley, Katherine et al. (2012), *Department of defense energy initiatives: Background and issues for congress*. Congressional Research Service. Available at: http://fas.org/sgp/crs/natsec/R42558.pdf Access date: 10 June 2019.

SIPRI (2019a), Military expenditure database. Available at: https://www.sipri.org/databases/milex Access date: 10 June 2019.

SIPRI (2019b), Trends in international transfers of major weapons. Available at: https://www.sipri.org/gallery/arms-transfers-graphics-0 Access date: 10 June 2019.

Steffen, Will, Rockström, Johan, et al. (2018), Trajectories of the earth system in the anthropocene. In: *PNAS Perspective*, 115, 33, 8252–8259.

Tian, Nan, Fleurant, Aude, et al. (2019), Trends in military expenditure, 2018. SIPRI. Available at: https://www.sipri.org/sites/default/files/2019-04/fs_1904_milex_2018.pdf Access date: 10 June 2019.

Unmussig, Barbara (2018), Una visió radicalment realista del clima. Ara. Available at: https://www.ara.cat/opinio/barbara-unmussig-visio-radicalment-realista-clima_0_2121388066.html?_ga=2.58512554.1076684043.1546531836-1462874421.1520091862 Access date: 10 June 2019.

Vitali, Stefania, Glattfelder, James B. et al. (2011), The network of global corporate control. In: *PLoS ONE*, 6, 10. Available at: https://journals.plos.org/plosone/article?id=10.1371/journal.pone.0025995

War Resisters International (2019), Why is action on militarism essential to action on climate change? Available at https://www.wri-irg.org/en/story/2019/why-action-militarism-essential-action-climate-change Access date: 10 June 2019.

8 Peace movement work on military spending

Colin Archer

8.1 Introduction

Militarism is a big beast. How to hunt it down or at least tame it? Peace movements over the last two centuries have struggled to find the most effective answers. Or to switch the metaphor: it is a mighty tree in a forest of social ills. Is it best brought down by quickly chopping off all its twigs and branches, or can the trunk be axed? Better still, could the whole structure be uprooted? Substitute diverse weapons systems and specific wars for branches; and fundamental causes (inequality, colonialism, machismo, xenophobia, etc.) for the roots, and the significance of the image may become clearer.

Around the world many peace campaigners continue to feel that the economic dimension represents the trunk of the tree, and as such is a potent area for struggle against the war system. The economic aspect includes arms research, production and trade; military spending by governments; and indeed the capitalist system itself, seen by many as generative of violent conflict.

We shall focus here primarily on military spending, though with some references to related topics, notably the weapons business and disarmament proposals.

8.2 Historical perspective

8.2.1 From 1815 to 1850

Writings against war and in praise of peace are found already in ancient/classical eras and are embedded in all faith traditions. It is worth recalling too that many of the peasants' revolts in the medieval period were protests against taxation and conscription imposed by kings and feudal lords in order to supply them with the resources to pursue their armed quarrels – and so were in some sense 'peace protests'. Though not a peasants' revolt, this grievance was an important element of the celebrated Magna Carta of 1215, imposed on King John by the English barons.

However, historians date the beginning of the organised peace movement to 1815 (exactly 600 years later), when the first peace societies were set up in

New York and London. Their roots were in the anti-slavery movement, and also drew on an awareness of a general sense of social and economic exhaustion following the long-running Napoleonic Wars. In the British case the original impulses were religious (several Quakers were among the founders). The influence of these UK/US pioneers spread to other parts of Europe by the 1830s. By this point the military spending theme ('guns or butter') appears to have become central to the general case for peace:

> The promise of reduced armories, of militias replacing professional and conscripted forces, of the conversion of armaments plants into factories for civilian goods attracted adherents on the Continent from the time of the Napoleonic Wars down to the very last moment of peace on 31 July 1914.
>
> (Cooper, 1991)

To this was added the proposal to oblige banks to refuse war loans. 'My object is to promote peace by withholding the sinews of war' declared Richard Cobden, the celebrated Manchester MP and campaigner.

In the 1840s and 1850s he and others introduced a further economic theme to the debate: free trade, presented as a bulwark against war. The proposition was that the more a nation engaged in commerce with other states, the more likely it was to develop cooperative relations rather than warlike ones. Cobden was influenced in this by Adam Smith, the great apostle of free trade. This argument was given powerful expression by the Nobel laureate Norman Angell in his 1910 work *The Great Illusion*. However, Britain's vigorous trade with Germany in the early 20th century evidently failed to prevent the First World War from breaking out.

In 1843 the first Universal Peace Congress was held in London, bringing together 324 peace activists from several countries. Its demands included arbitration, an international court, and…cuts in military expenditure. This position, reaffirmed again at the Paris congress of 1849, reflected in part the influence of Jean-Jacques de Sellon of the Geneva Peace Society; St Simonians in France such as Eugénie Niboyet; the economist Frédéric Bastiat, the journalist Emile de Girardin and above all the great Victor Hugo himself. But the movement was already past its mid-century peak, following the revolutions of 1848 and the counter-revolutions of 1849. These tumultuous events were followed by the Crimean War, other European conflicts and the American Civil War – all of which confronted peace movements with the difficulty of their task and tended to lead to nationalism-related divisions.

8.2.2 *From 1850 to 1870*

This era saw the splits in peace movement crystallise into two main tendencies: on the one hand, a conservative wing led by Passy and Cobden; and on the other, a radical faction focussing on national liberation and human rights, and tending to favour anticlericalism and conditional, rather than absolute, pacifism. This position was typified by the fiery Garibaldi, and reflected also the rise of early socialist and working-class agitation, as well as the first stirrings of the women's peace movement (Liddington, 1989).

8.2.3 From 1870 to 1914

The period following the Franco-Prussian War – a major trauma for Europeans – proved to be an era with a sharply divided character. It saw an impressive growth of progressive thinking and the spread of peace movements; their coordination through the establishment of the International Peace Bureau (1891); and the introduction of the Nobel prizes (1901). It also reflected the dominance in intellectual circles of a fervent social optimism based on faith in rationalism, the remarkable advances in science and technology, and the apparent acceptance by elites, even heads of state (for example, at the Hague Peace Conferences of 1899 and 1907) of a positive peace philosophy. In retrospect it was a golden era. Paradoxically, it was also a period in which a generalised spurt in aggressive nationalism was bolstered by a major arms race. The result was world war – as foreseen by the great peace advocate Bertha von Suttner, and the influential economist of future wars, Jean de Bloch. The efforts of Jean Jaurès and especially French MPs via the Inter-Parliamentary Union to condemn the arms race came to nothing.

An indication of the extent to which peace movement ideas on the economic dimension had been accepted in the pre-war period by at least one part of the establishment is shown vividly in materials on the British parliamentary debate on military spending, collected by the Arming All Sides project, a historical study by the Campaign Against the Arms Trade:

> As Parliament debated the 1905 Finance Bill Liberal politicians argued to reduce defence expenditure, arguing that government funds should be diverted towards social reform. In the 1906 General Election the Liberal Party won a majority, and subsequently introduced wide ranging education, health and welfare reforms including free school meals for some children, attempts to increase the numbers of children in secondary education and pensions for those over 70 years old [...]
>
> Northamptonshire MP Francis Channing argued: 'Allowing for the repayment of capital charges for military and naval works, the total expenditure on war and armaments during the last ten years amounted to something like £400,000,000. Through the policy of war, expansion, and reckless Imperialism, the whole of that money had been thrown into the sea.'
>
> Another Liberal, Joseph Walton, wanted more money spent on education and less on the military. Education spending had increased by £6,000,000 while spending on the Army and Navy had grown from £35,500,000 to £71,250,000, he said. This reminded him of an incident at a Scotch election, where the candidate was heckled by being

asked, 'Am I to understand, Sorr, that whilst you are prepared to spend £31,000,000 over the Army and Navy, you are only willin' to spend £8,000,000 on education – that is, £31,000,000 for blawin' brains oot and only £8,000,000 for pittin' brains in?'[...]

In 1909, introducing a new budget, Liberal Prime Minister David Lloyd George said: 'This is a war budget. It is for raising money to wage implacable warfare against poverty and squalidness. Only six years later, he would be heading the Ministry of Munitions, aiming to ensure the supply of armaments for a different kind of war'.

(Arming All Sides, 2020)

8.2.4 From 1919 to 1939

The peace movement picked itself up after the disaster of the 'Great War' by pouring its hope into the newly established League of Nations and the arbitration mechanism that had been set up by the Hague Conferences. Never again! was the heartfelt slogan that resounded across the continent. It was not long before the finger of blame began to be pointed at what became known as 'merchants of death' – the arms dealers. There had in fact been warnings before and during the war on this specific topic. The British socialist G.H. Perris drew on the work of Liebknecht and Delaisi to compile a devastating report for the 1913 Universal Peace Congress documenting the influence of arms manufacturers in fuelling the arms race and blatantly stimulating nationalistic militarism. Congress resolutions also condemned the role of banks in funding loans for war products. 'The French delegate, Jeanne Mélin, contrasted the largesse of banks lending money for war with their miserly rejection of funding for social needs at home' (Cortright, 2008: 97).

A major development during the First World War was the historic 1915 Hague conference of women. At the end of the Congress, a set of resolutions were adopted with regard to seven different subjects: women and war, actions towards peace, principles of a permanent peace, international cooperation, the education of children, women and the peace settlement conference and lastly a resolution stating the actions to be taken after the congress. Under International Cooperation, the section on General Disarmament focussed on the need for states to collectively take over the arms trade: '(The Congress) sees in the private profits accruing from the great armaments factories a powerful hindrance to the abolition of war' (International Congress of Woman, 1915).

The post-war backlash against war profiteers reached far beyond the pacifist and socialist activists. Powerful critiques were issued even by high-level figures such as Admiral Wemyss and Lord Welby, who declared:

We are in the hands of an organisation of crooks. They are politicians, generals, manufacturers of armaments and journalists. All of them are anxious for unlimited expenditure, and go on inventing scares to terrify the public.

(Noel-Baker, 1937)

In the USA, such concerns were given formal and detailed analysis through the Nye Hearings in the US Senate in 1934–1935. 'Arms manufacturers were grilled about the enormous profits they reaped in a war that left more than 50,000 troops dead...The hearings ...were fed by and helped nourish an unprecedented wave of anti-corporate sentiment' (Cortright, 2008). Cortright points out that the hearings were largely a peace movement initiative, notably the result of efforts by Dorothy Detzer, a skilled lobbyist from the Women's International League for Peace and Freedom. Their conclusions were echoed in 1935 by a similar Royal Commission in the UK.

It should be noted, however, that the focus of this anti-war revulsion was mostly on the private sector rather than government allocations. The latter theme had already been raised at the 1932 World Disarmament Conference, even though the meeting itself was a failure. The UK refused to contemplate general disarmament, and Germany simply walked out. Fascism was on the rise, and rearmament was soon to begin on all sides.

8.2.5 From 1945 to 1990

The post-Second World War period was different to that following the First World War. True, there was hope for a peaceful world under the auspices of the new United Nations, and for some in the movement, the dream of a world government or a form of world federalism. But the optimism was bitterly short-lived. By 1949 the Cold War was taking shape, with the founding of NATO and six years later, the Warsaw Pact. The peace movement was once again split, this time on very sharp ideological lines. The Soviet-sponsored World Peace Council was formally constituted in 1950, and attracted support from across the Communist world. 'Non-aligned' peace movements were affiliated to a range of peace internationals, mostly with Western orientation, though critical of their own governments.

Nuclear armament was the great game-changer. The threat of mutual – or indeed universal – destruction was sufficiently serious, and at times immediate, for it to become the largest single focus of peace activity for the next 40 years. The cost of nuclear weapons was a theme in the disarmament struggle, but not primary.

What emerged instead was a critique of what came to be known as the military-industrial complex (MIC) – especially in the USA, where the size of the complex dwarfed any other.

The critique drew on earlier analyses but gained popularity in the wake of the 1955 AFSC (Quaker) report Speak Truth to Power. The insights embodied in the report gained a far greater audience with the now-famous Eisenhower farewell speech in 1961:

> We have been compelled to create a permanent armaments industry of vast proportions. Added to this, three and a half million men and women are directly engaged in the defense establishment. We annually spend

on military security alone more than the net income of all United States corporations.... In the councils of government, we must guard against the acquisition of unwarranted influence, whether sought or unsought, by the military-industrial complex. The potential for the disastrous rise of misplaced power exists and will persist.

(Eisenhower, 1961)

In fact, Eisenhower had already made an even more trenchant argument, against military spending, in his 1953 speech to the American Society of Newspaper Editors:

Every gun that is made, every warship launched, every rocket fired signifies, in the final sense, a theft from those who hunger and are not fed, those who are cold and are not clothed. This world in arms is not spending money alone. It is spending the sweat of its laborers, the genius of its scientists, the hopes of its children. The <u>cost</u> of one modern heavy bomber is this: a modern brick school in more than 30 cities. It is two electric power plants, each serving a town of 60,000 population. It is two fine, fully equipped hospitals. It is some fifty miles of concrete pavement. We pay for a single fighter with a half-million bushels of wheat. We pay for a single <u>destroyer</u> with new homes that could have housed more than 8,000 people.... This is not a way of life at all, in any true sense. Under the cloud of threatening war, it is humanity hanging from a cross of iron.

(Eisenhower, 1953)

The critique was further advanced in 1965 with the publication of an important article 'Is there a Military Industrial Complex which prevents peace?' (Pilisuk and Hayden), which was highly influential with the anti-war movement, arguing that 'American society IS a military-industrial complex'. Among the many subsequent analysts of the war system and the nefarious linkages between the arms industry and government are Anatol Rapaport, Richard J Barnett, Fred Cook and Chalmers Johnson.

But it was not simply the size and influence of the MIC that disturbed pacifists and progressives alike. It was also the uses to which it was being put overseas. In 1950–1953 the USA became bogged down in the Korean War, then even more deeply in SE Asia. The thrust towards foreign interventions and adventures continued through the latter part of the Cold War (Central America, Middle East, etc.) and persists today in the wake of the Somali, Afghan, Iraqi and other conflicts. All have elicited protests, and in some cases prolonged opposition movements.

Opposition to military spending can be located as one component of this broader critique. The late 1960s and 1970s saw the rise of a huge anti-war movement in the USA and beyond, which itself was simply part of a highly diversified counter-culture. The period saw the rise of multiple and overlapping social movements: civil rights/anti-racism, women's and gay liberation, environmental, etc.

A good example of the new militancy is the Port Huron Statement, a 1962 political manifesto of Students for a Democratic Society. This wide-ranging statement, drafted by the late Tom Hayden, included a 'New Left' analysis of the Pentagon and the whole US political-economic system. It offered a robust critique of imperialism, military interventions and their justifications (which at that time meant 'the Communist threat'; later, post-9/11, becoming 'Terrorism'). Among other targets, the Statement attacked the permanent war economy, the concentration of defence spending among a few giant corporations, the large numbers of defence-dependent jobs and the triangular relations of business, military and political spheres. It rejected 'A fiscal policy based upon defense expenditures as pump-priming 'public works' – without a significant emphasis on peaceful "public works" to meet social priorities and alleviate personal hardships' (Students for a Democratic Society, 1964).

Prior to 1975, the single biggest task of the Movement (as it was known) was to secure US withdrawal from Vietnam and SE Asia. Once Reagan was installed in the White House in 1979, a whole range of other challenges emerged, notably the dangers of a renewed nuclear arms race with the USSR. Huge mobilisations were organised across the world in the early 1980s, the largest of which was the one million + demonstration in Central Park, NY in 1982, at the time of the UN Second Special Session on Disarmament.

In the USA, the largest movement was the Nuclear Freeze campaign. In Europe the focus was the Euromissiles (Cruise, Pershing and the Soviet SS20s) that threatened the very survival of Europe and indeed the planet itself. A vast biodiversity of organisations and ad hoc movements sprang up and coalesced in protest gatherings both large and small. Two particular developments were significant: first, the END network that tried – and at times succeeded – in linking activists on both sides of the Berlin Wall in an effort to 'dissolve the blocs'; and second, the celebrated women's camp at the Greenham Common air base in the UK, which offered a day-by-day gendered rebuke to the militarists. Protests were felt and heard far beyond N. America and Europe. The US historian Lawrence S. Wittner (2009) documents the global nuclear disarmament movement in his magisterial three-volume work.

While the critique of military spending was somewhat submerged during the Cold War, it did surface in a number of places. One of these was the US network known as Mobilization for Survival (MfS or MOBE), established in 1977 and dissolved in 1992. This was a national organisation comprising affiliated grassroots peace and social justice groups working to: abolish nuclear weapons and power; stop military intervention; reverse the arms race; meet human needs. MfS' primary focus was to nurture grassroots movements by reaching out to community-based organisations, and providing resources and assistance. MfS promoted a wide range of protest and educational activities, and also published a quarterly newsletter, 'The Mobilizer'.

The spending critique also featured in the efforts of trade union organisations seeking to find alternative work for members engaged in military and/or nuclear industries. One highlight of this movement was the unsuccessful but highly inspirational work of the Lucas Aerospace Shop Stewards and their Alternative Corporate Plan featuring products to meet civilian need in replacement of the defence-related orders they were fulfilling at the time (Salisbury, 1976).

At another level entirely, the period is notable for a whole series of UN resolutions and proposals promoting reduced military spending and conversion. Mostly these were passed at the General Assembly and were not implemented.

When the UN was founded in 1945 the two principal tasks assigned to it were international security and the promotion of development. The relationship between these two issues – often referred to as 'disarmament and development' – has received much attention since that time. The classical statement of the UN's intent is enshrined in the Charter:

> In order to promote the establishment and maintenance of international peace and security with the least diversion for armaments of the world's human and economic resources, the Security Council shall be responsible for formulating, with the assistance of the Military Staff Committee referred to in article 47, plans to be submitted to the members of the United Nations for the establishment of a system for the regulation of armaments.
>
> (UN Charter, Art.26)

In 1987 the UN convened a specific Conference on Disarmament and Development, whose central theme was reallocating military budgets.

A number of political leaders are associated with these efforts, notably Alfonso Garcia-Robles, Alva Myrdal, Inga Thorsson, Oscar Arias, Sean MacBride, Jayantha Dhanapala and many others (Archer and Hay-Edie, 2006). Such moves were partly the result of popular protest at the risks and intensification of the Cold War, together with the persistence of poverty on a massive scale amid a fast-growing world economy favouring the rich. They also reflected the work of researchers in the advancing field of peace studies, for example, at Stockholm International Peace Research Institute (SIPRI), and the popularisation of their findings by authors such as Ruth Leger Sivard.

8.2.6 *From 1990 to 2001*

The end of the Cold War gave way to a particularly complex decade. Loss of peace movement momentum due to the end of East-West confrontations and the immediate nuclear threat was accompanied by a diversification of focus. Human rights, social development, environment and more all absorbed activist energies and favoured new coalitions and political formations. These issues were highlighted by a remarkable series of major UN Summits, culminating in the Millennium Declaration and ultimately the Sustainable Development Goals (2015).

Few thought that armed conflict would evaporate. New crises emerged but in geographically limited areas: Rwanda, the Balkans, Sri Lanka, etc. The UN published its vision in the pathbreaking Agenda for Peace (1991), but overall the role of UN was disappointing, mainly owing to the reluctance of major states to tackle challenging problems and to give the UN the resources and authority it needed.

Nevertheless, hopes were high for a worldwide shift in priorities, given the drop in military spending in the early 1990s. The conventional wisdom is that the long-hoped-for 'peace dividend' never materialised. However, an important argument has been made by the Nobel laureate economist Lawrence Klein. He argues that after the Cold War, the substantial cuts in US military spending led to a reduced deficit which, when combined with a tight lid on other government spending, gave rise to a significant drop in interest rates.

> Not only did conventional capital formation move ahead, but venture capital for the new technologies was forthcoming. The US economy ultimately enjoyed the combination of unprecedented expansion of employment, (with [joblessness] down to less than 4%), high productivity gains, low inflation and all the 'butter' the civilians could absorb.... In the 1990s, the US became the principal locomotive of the world economy.
>
> (Klein, 2004)

In other words, there was a kind of peace dividend – but it was private sector-led, and in fact it did more to increase inequalities than to reduce them.

Another buzzword in this period was Human Security. The concept was first promoted widely by the UN Development Programme in its 1994 Human Development report. This was helpful in challenging the military-led notion of 'national security' but ultimately little support was found at government level for any mutually agreed constraints on military expenditure. The best achievement in this direction was what is now known as the UN Annual Report on Military Expenditure – a transparency instrument only.

One positive feature of the post-Cold War years was conversion, notably of military bases formerly used by the Soviet Union in East Germany, and some US bases and facilities in the continental USA. As Miriam Pemberton of Institute for Policy Studies (IPS) reports:

> Since the 1970s a small office within the Pentagon, the Office of Economic Adjustment, has offered planning grants and technical assistance to help military-dependent communities develop their own strategies to capitalize on existing economic strengths and adjust to postwar economic conditions (CITE) and in bibliography.

More recently the Pentagon set up a Base Realignment and Closure (BRAC) programme. During the BRAC rounds of 1988, 1991, 1993, 1995 and 2005, over 350 installations were closed. However, whether this can be considered military conversion to civilian use depends on the new uses to which the facilities were put. It is worth noting that in many cases, the closures and alternative uses were secured through broad cooperation between local and national authorities working with labour unions, researchers and community/ peace activists.

Then-acting budget chief of the Department of Defense John Roth stated: 'Twenty percent of the Pentagon's facilities could be closed without negative impact'. However, the process can become highly politicised, as lawmakers see bases and ports in their districts as vulnerable to budget cuts, which would affect the local economy greatly – and therefore weaken their political support. As a result, Congress has rejected every Pentagon request for new closings since 2005.

8.2.7 From 2001 to 2019

History is a twisting road and the 9/11 attacks constituted another turning point of great significance. They re-framed the concept of 'enemy' for the Western world and became the justification for two major wars, in Afghanistan and Iraq. They thus provided a new impetus for US-led military strategies, forces, interventions...and spending. The post-Cold War drop in military expenditure levels was reversed. At the same time, rising powers, especially in Asia, were getting into the military game in a big way. The USA is now the largest, but far from the only, big spender. We are now in a globalised war economy.

On the positive side, the huge global mobilisation in February 2013 against war in Iraq was arguably the largest simultaneous demonstration in history. It failed to prevent the invasion, but undoubtedly had an inspirational effect on those who launched the Arab Spring several years later. Meanwhile the World Social Forums and the Occupy movements did much to infuse a new spirit of contestation and connectedness into civil society activity. Their critique of globalisation (sometimes) included rejection of war and militarism. Finally, it can be argued that – for good or ill – the arrival of electronic and now social media have set in motion the biggest revolution in activist practice and methodology since the invention of the printing press.

8.3 IPB and the global campaign on military spending

In the post-9/11 period, the International Peace Bureau (IPB) took up the theme of Human Security as an alternative perspective on counter-terrorism. This shift in organisational priorities was already evident during the major five-day conference on A World Without Violence, held in Barcelona in 2004. One full day of this ambitious programme was devoted to the Economy of War.

The success of the event (there were 1,000 participants) encouraged a major review of IPB campaigning priorities. This identified a crucial space in the international peace movement landscape. It is important to note that up to this point there had been no international campaign network on the issue of governmental military spending. Substantial amounts of research had been done (and continues to this day) among academic institutions and some NGOs, and there had been many general denunciations of the size of the commitment to the military and the opportunity costs. But there had been no intentional, structured global campaign linking pressure groups and protesters.

The first stage was the creation of the Disarmament for Development (D for D) campaign. The title was a more pro-active variant on the UN term 'Disarmament and Development' which implied conceptual and policy linkages in both directions.

IPB identified three 'baskets' of concerns: (1) Military expenditure versus social spending; (2) Effects of militarism on development and (3) Justifications for military expenditure.

Two books were published to provide an intellectual toolbox for campaigners around the world: *Warfare or Welfare?* (Archer and Hay-Edie, 2006) and *Whose Priorities?* (Archer, 2007). Both books provide examples of creative campaigning by NGOs and other civil society organisations that have taken up these issues. More recent IPB publications focus on the links between military spending and the Development Agenda of the United Nations (SDGs), as well as the challenge of climate change. These, in turn, were followed by Nuclear Weapons at What Cost? (Cramer, 2009). This work builds on both Atomic Audit (Schwartz, 1998) and Audit atomique (Barrillot, 1999), which analyse the data on the financial costs of nuclear weapons programmes in the USA and France. IPB's work was the first global analysis of this. A more recent addition to the campaign literature is the *GCOMS Handbook* (Global Campaign on Military Spending, 2018).

In 2009, during the IPB conference in Washington DC, discussions were held with key figures in the US movement, notably at the Institute for Policy Studies (IPS), regarding plans for a Global Day (now Days) of Action on Military Spending (GDAMS). Meanwhile, IPB staff began forging links with the Stockholm International Peace Research Institute (SIPRI) – especially around alignment of the GDAMS date/s with the publication of SIPRI's annual military spending statistics. The following 12 months allowed time for the necessary groundwork to be done, and in 2011 IPB and IPS jointly launched the first round of GDAMS. In 2014 the IPB was ready to expand the initiative to a year-round effort: the Global Campaign on Military Spending (GCOMS).

GDAMS actions initially took place during a single day, and subsequently during a short period in April-May – normally including the US Tax Day and the SIPRI data release, which both help draw a lot of public attention to the issue around the world. Over time, new partnerships have been formed and new issues incorporated. In particular, the Paris Climate Change agreement (COP21) and (also in 2015) the adoption of the Sustainable Development Goals (SDGs) by the UN have offered important opportunities to make the link to other global issues. IPB and its GCOMS partners have consistently supported the notion that much of the money locked into the military sector should and – given political will – could be made available for such purposes.

By the end of 2015 it was becoming clear that a third area would also be requiring major investments: humanitarian crises. This issue was addressed in the May 2016 World Humanitarian Summit (WHS) in Istanbul.

A major milestone for the D for D programme was the International Conference 'Disarm! For a Climate of Peace' held in Berlin in 2016. Organised by the International Peace Bureau, it brought together a wide variety of experts and advocates from all around the world, with over 1,000 participants from 58 different countries. Four Nobel Peace laureates participated in the conference. Campaigning on military spending was the most prominent theme and was highlighted in detail in the IPB Action Agenda adopted at the conference. (Braun et al., 2018) A follow-up conference is planned for 2021 in Barcelona. In 2017, the GCOMS headquarters was transferred from Geneva to Barcelona.

One of the key developments in 2018 was the launch of a second annual GCOMS campaign focus. Cut Milex is a fall/autumn mobilisation, aiming to influence the military spending debate in Parliaments. With actions mainly during October and December, it coincides with the parliamentary discussion period of national budgets in many countries. The Cut Milex campaign carries several main messages:

1   To reduce military spending while redirecting its funds to social needs, cooperation, conflict mediation and peace building.
2   To increase transparency and avoid opacity in official data on exports and military and defence industry.
3   To introduce criteria for addressing military spending in national budgets in a comprehensive and rigorous way.
4   To ensure that arms programmes are audited and controlled by the nation's parliament.

8.4 Other initiatives

While GCOMS is the broadest global campaign network encompassing military spending as a whole, other related efforts have been established in recent years – work on which the GCOMS actively builds – such as:

1   The Abolition 2000 working group on economic dimensions of militarism which was established at the Abolition 2000 annual meeting held in Geneva in September 2011. Abolition 2000 is a global network of

activists working for the elimination of nuclear weapons. The working group focusses on cutting nuclear weapons budgets and shifting this funding to meet social, economic and environmental needs. It provides an umbrella for work done in both nuclear-armed and non-nuclear countries, and challenges both public and private investments in nuclear armaments.[1] The group combines the approaches of two earlier Abolition 2000 Working Groups: Divestment and Military Corporate. The latter was the work of the International Network on Disarmament and Globalization. Its convenor, Steve Staples, writes:

> The Working Group was a trailblazer in building the analytical connections between militarism and neo-liberal globalization – especially around the period of the late 1990s when the anti-corporate globalization movement was at its zenith. At the landmark anti-WTO protests in Seattle in November 1999, Abolition 2000 hosted an important event titled The WTO and the Global War System.

While much of the Network's efforts were focussed on corporate/private sector involvement with militarism, they also highlighted the 'security exception', which shields the war industry from challenges by the World Trade Organization to state subsidies. Article XXI of the GATT, the principal agreement of the WTO, allows governments' free rein for actions taken to protect national security interests. This actually spurs government military spending, since only military spending is free from challenges. The consequence is that governments are obliged to use the military sector when seeking to promote jobs, new emerging industries or high-tech manufacturing.

2   The Move the Nuclear Weapons Money campaign, which was launched in October 2016 at the 135th Inter-Parliamentary Union Assembly, by the Basel Peace Office, International Peace Bureau, World Future Council and Parliamentarians for Nuclear Non-proliferation and Disarmament. It now includes a number of other organisations and networks including the Global Security Institute, Peace Accelerators, UNFOLD ZERO, World Federalist Movement and the Abolition 2000 Working Group on Economic Dimensions of Nuclearism. The publication *Move the Nuclear Weapons Money: A handbook for civil society and legislators* (IPB, 2016) has proved to be a key reference work.

During 2019, the agendas of peace movements across the world increasingly became focussed on linkages to the separate but related issue of climate change. While most climate activists have tended to ignore the peace dimension, the conflict risks associated with extreme climate changes are becoming well known. Less attention has been given to the evidence of the carbon emissions of the military, and its diversion of major public resources away from climate adaptation. This therefore presents a major campaigning opportunity for activists in the GCOMS and related movements over the coming years.

8.5 The campaign goes global

Most of peace movement history (and certainly most of the work on military expenditure) has taken place in the developed world, especially Europe and USA. This is due to a number of factors: democratic space is vital for the flourishing of critical peace movement work; these were in any case the big-spending countries; civil society in poor countries has tended to focus on national independence and development, not militarism. Some states rejected restrictions on arms trade as discriminatory (until the start of the Arms Trade Treaty process).

However, since the end of the Cold War new peace-related currents have emerged in the Global South, a phenomenon explicable by the relaxation of the superpower grip on political developments; the rise of certain dominant states (for example, BRICS) leading to concerns regarding their military capacities – not least on account of their repressive internal role; a new focus by international civil society on issues affecting developing countries and conflict zones: small arms, landmines and cluster munitions, conventional weapons, war crimes, as well as wider issues of internal conflicts, human rights abuses and development. Military expenditure also falls into this category. Ongoing armed conflicts (whether they involve external actors or not) and their associated load of human suffering, which have focussed academic and activist minds on the causes, and also the beneficiaries, of militarism. The intensification of globalisation has generated new critiques and modes of resistance, notably in the Global South. Military expenditure is one aspect of the neoliberal economic model. Sometimes it is a matter of the privatisation of arms industry, sometimes the latter is run directly by the state, or the military carve out large areas of the civilian economy (Siddiqa, 2016). In several major states the aim is to 'indigenise' weapons production rather than continue to import.

Despite these shifts, GDAMS/GCOMS partners are still primarily located in the Global North. There is, however, strong participation in Asia – notably in Japan, S. Korea and the Philippines. A key element of the challenge of building this worldwide effort is to identify and support new partners in Africa, the Middle East and Latin America.

The number of campaign actions organised each year has usually exceeded 100 events in 30 or more countries. A whole range of actions have been organised, including street protests/demonstrations, seminars, press conferences, media releases, videos, declarations, petitions, peace vigils, 'penny polls' and photo-shoots. Equally diverse are the linkages made with regional, national and local issues. These include the SDGs, humanitarian disasters, militarisation and drug wars in Latin America, the Eurozone crisis in Europe, nuclear weapons modernisation, the tendency towards militarism in Japan, the growing tension between South and North Korea and other issues.

8.6 Conclusion

Looking back across two hundred years of organised peace movement campaigning, it is striking how persistent is the focus on military spending. It was not always the top priority of the main movements, but it has been widely understood to be a key aspect of popular opposition to militarism and war. However, the widespread perception that far too much of the public purse was spent on war preparations was often articulated only at the rhetorical level, without any real political impact. It has always been difficult to interrogate the complex underlying causes and drivers of militarisation. Hence the importance of the GCOMS in offering structure, international coordination, resources and continuity to diverse and sporadic peace protests.

Much more remains to be done, notably in reaching out to other sectors of society and building an effective lobbying force. Since budget decisions are made largely at the national level, it is appropriate, indeed highly necessary, to forge national coalitions to impact such decisions. The unprecedented mobilisation of young people around the issue of climate change offers an ideal opportunity to engage a new generation of activists in this work. But by framing the issue widely, in terms of potential benefit to the whole of society, GCOMS also offers a series of exciting partnership possibilities with social change actors from all walks of life and varied political perspectives.

Note

1 For list of campaign actions undertaken by various groups, and related resources, see: http://www.abolition2000.org/en/working-groups/economic -dimensions-of-nuclearism-working-group/.

Bibliography

Archer, C. (2007), *Whose priorities? A guide for campaigners on military and social spending.* Geneva, International Peace Bureau.

Archer, C. and Hay-Edie, D. (2006), *Warfare or welfare? Disarmament for development in the 21st century: A human security approach.* Geneva, International Peace Bureau.

Archer, C. and Willi, A. (2012), *Opportunity costs: Military spending and the UN development agenda.* Geneva, International Peace Bureau.

Arming All Sides (2020), Blowing brains out or putting them in?, Available in https://armingallsides.org.uk/case_studies/blowing-brains-out-or-putting-them-in/, Accessed 10/01/2020

Barrillot, B. (1999), *Audit atomique: le coût de l'arsenal nucléaire français, 1945–2010.* France, CRDPC.

Braun, R. et al. (2018), *Disarmament, peace and development. Vol. 27, contributions to conflict management, peace economics and development.* UK, Emerald Publishing.

Carter, A. (1992), *Peace movements: International protest and world politics since 1945*. UK, Longman.

Cooper, S. (1991), *Patriotic pacifism, waging war on war in Europe, 1815–1914*. New York, Oxford University Press.

Cortright, D. (2008), *Peace: A History of Movements and Ideas*, Cambridge, Cambridge University Press.

Cramer, B. (2009), *Nuclear weapons at what cost?* Geneva, International Peace Bureau.

Eisenhower (1953), Address to the American Society of Newspaper Editors delivered 16 April 1953, Statler Hotel, Washington, D.C. Available in https://www.americanrhetoric.com/speeches/dwighteisenhowercrossofiron.htm, Accessed 23/12/2019

Eisenhower (1961), Transcript of President Dwight D. Eisenhower's Farewell Address (1961), Available in https://www.ourdocuments.gov/doc.php?flash=true&doc=90&page=transcript, Accessed 23/12/2019

Enomoto, T. (ed.) (2017), *Disarmament and arms control in the history of international politics: From the 19th century to the present*. Tokyo, Nihon Keizai Hyoron Sha.

Gittings, J. (2012), *The glorious art of peace*. Oxford, Oxford University Press.

Global Campaign on Military Spending (2018). *GCOMS Handbook*. Centre Delàs d'Estudis per la Pau and International Peace Bureau, Barcelona.

International Congress of Women (1915), Report of the International Congress of Women, The Hague, Women's Peace Party.

IPB, PNND, WFC (2016), *Move the nuclear weapons money: A handbook for civil society and* legislators. International Peace Bureau, Parliamentarians for Nuclear Non-proliferation and Disarmament, and the World Future Council, Geneva.

Klein, L. (2004), *World peace and economic prosperity,* presented to the UN Symposium on Disarmament and Development.

Liddington, J. (1989), *The long road to greenham: Feminism and anti-militarism in Britain since 1820*. London, Virago.

Lorincz, T. (2014), *Demilitarization for deep decarbonization: Reducing militarism and military expenditures to invest in the UN green climate fund and to create low-carbon economies and resilient communities*, Geneva, International Peace Bureau.

Melman, S. (1985), *The permanent defense economy*, New York, Simon & Schuster.

Noel-Baker, P. (1937), *The private manufacture of armaments*, London, OUP.

Salisbury, B. (1976), Story of the Lucas Plan, Available in http://lucasplan.org.uk/-story-of-the-lucas-plan/, Accessed 4/01/2020

Schwartz, S. (1998), *Atomic audit: The costs and consequences of U.S. nuclear weapons since 1940*, Washington, DC, Brookings Institution.

Siddiqa, A. (2016), *Military Inc: Inside Pakistan's military economy*, London, Pluto Press.

Sivard, R. (1996), *World military and social expenditures*, (16 editions, from 1974 to 1996), Washington, DC, World Priorities Inc.

Students for a Democratic Society (1964): The Port Huron Statement, New York, Available in http://www.progressivefox.com/misc_documents/PortHuronStatement.pdf, Accessed 3/01/2020

Swanson, D. (ed) (2011), *The military industrial complex at 50*, Charlottesville, VA, davidswanson.org.

Wittner, L. (2009), *Confronting the bomb*, Stanford, CA, Stanford University Press (summary volume).

9 Conclusion

Jordi Calvo Rufanges

Security and military spending form an inseparable partnership in which security, despite being within the scope of political science, is a highly complex issue, while military expenditure stems from political decisions in the purest sense. Military expenses depend solely on those public-spending budgets that are put forward by governments on an annual basis and, where appropriate, they are debated and supported at a parliamentary level. Security, however, is part of a continuous analysis, not only of experts in the field, but when understood in a broad manner, it is a subject of shared debate within a society.

In this publication we have focussed on an analysis of security from a more traditional standpoint, State security, or "national security". This concept is commonly referred to as Homeland Security, an Anglo-Saxon term that after the attacks of 9/11 formed a new national security strategy that originated in the USA, and which has spread throughout the world with the doctrine of the War on Terror. In this concept the internal security of a country and the defence of its external borders are interlocked in such a way that the frontier that theoretically separates them is often blurred.

Security has become a focus of aspirations, and it is one that is coveted, not only in the eyes of everyday internal security departments, but also by the departments of Intelligence and Defence, and in such a way that security forces, intelligence centres and military personnel become jumbled together in a mixed bag of public resources that are all related to security.

The first aspect to consider is that of accurately quantifying a country's military spending, and of all countries as a whole, and this is necessary for two important reasons. The first relates to the capacity for analysis as possessed by the militarizing processes of international relations, which are essential in any political analysis, whether it focusses on peace, or conflict. The second reason involves militarized responses to the internal security issues of each country; from the use of military capabilities and those methods used to deal with organized crime, or other common illegal actions, to securitizing responses made with regard to aspects of a human, social or environmental nature, such as those responses implemented with military means and modes to migration, health or climate crises.

Among all the criteria used, only one is accepted on an international basis, the reliability of which is determined by the independent nature of the institution that has drawn it up, the Stockholm International Peace Research Institute (SIPRI), which uses both experience and rigor in its calculations. Using those criteria that are limited to an analysis of defence ministry budgets is of little use, given that it is the habitual practice of governments to conceal various items of military expenditure items within the budgetary information of other ministries. The data from the SIPRI therefore reveals a sustained increase in world military spending from 9/11, whereas there was a marked overall reduction in military spending by the USSR after the fall of the Berlin Wall. Even the financial crisis of 2008 did not attain major reductions in military spending. All available data indicates that the War on Terror has had a significant impact on military budgets around the world, a war whose balance in terms of progress with respect to global peace and security could not be more negative. The world today is more insecure and there are greater restrictions on freedom than there were at the beginning of the millennium.

An increasing number of countries have chosen to advance their military capabilities since 9/11. The great military powers of Europe (Germany, the UK, France, Italy and Spain) have joined with the USA to make the area comprising NATO-member countries the most militarized zone in the world, one that accounts for over half of all global military expenditure every year. The fall of the Berlin Wall and the disappearance of bloc policy was not seen as a cue for NATO to reduce its military capabilities on the disappearance of the main threat to its security, it rather motivated the organization establish the region as that with the largest arsenals and arms industries in the world.

Nonetheless, it must be said that, either on their own initiative or in response to the military muscle displayed by NATO, the new great major economic powers, among which China and India are key players, have also invested large amounts of money in the development of important military capabilities. Russia has also sustained sufficient military expenditure to regain some of the international influence that it once enjoyed (although not without difficulties), however its budget accounts for just one-tenth of US military spending. Finally, the militarization of the Middle East is an example of an explosive combination of financial availability and geopolitical ambition, with the paradigmatic case of Saudi Arabia, whose military development, facilitated by massive exports from the USA and Western Europe, has reached a level that now enables it to undertake offensive military actions beyond its borders.

The development of military spending, arms exports and armed conflicts clearly coincides in all three cases. Their evolution follows similar trajectories over time, a fact that leads us to two possible conclusions. Either the existence of armed conflicts leads to increased expenditure in military budgets, in order to acquire the weapons with which to carry out those military operations associated with warfare, or alternatively, it is these enormous military budgets themselves that give rise to levels of militarization that are then used to make extensive use of military force in the pursuit of political objectives. It is highly probable that each case responds to a different scenario, and it is difficult to determine a pattern that explains the behaviour of these variables beyond the limits of the global data analysed here. An urgent reflection is necessary, and one that is also of an all-encompassing nature, in which the international community needs to curb the continued growth in the relationship between militarization and war, which is a catalyst for future conflicts.

This publication emphasizes the hegemonic and military leadership role of the West in recent decades, while remaining aware of the fact that international security is the responsibility of all states, and that no state with geopolitical relevance behaves any differently from any other like it. As previously mentioned, the USA has played a decisive role in shaping both the military framework and world conflict itself, with an imperialistic policy that has arisen from an overly optimistic and ambitious interpretation of the post-Cold War scenario. Its aim was nothing more than to maintain the worldwide dominance that it enjoyed after the Second World War. This supremacy was not only military, but also political and economic, given that under its control were the main global institutions that marshalled the process of globalization to the enormous benefit of the American business sector. A global domain of power that benefitted the American business sector more than any other actors.

The USA, however, has not been alone, either in terms of military escalation, or in the use of military operations abroad, nor for that matter in the development of its arms production industry. Western Europe has accompanied this process by playing a secondary role that legitimizes North America's strategy. First through its participation in the highly questionable military adventures that have taken place in Afghanistan, Iraq and Libya, and also in many other countries where terror has been used as an excuse to maintain or gain presence in places of geopolitical interest, or where a simple economic interest has been a key issue. Russia and China, each in their own sphere of influence, have followed the same example, intensifying the use of their own armed forces in order to gain access to territories whose economic and political value is beyond question. Examples of military missions, all of which have revealed the hypocrisy that underlies their implementation, and which may hardly be viewed as humanitarian, or as being justified under the doctrine of a responsibility to protect. Military missions that are finally shown to serve the overriding economic interests that require budgetary mechanisms free from the shackles of political debate.

The European Union has been the most recent player to board the militarization train. In the new multiannual financial framework of 2021–2027, and for the first time, a part of the European Community budget will be dedicated to defence-related issues. This, together with the urge to create a shared European security and defence policy, maps out a future in which the idea of a new European army looks ever more possible. This is a project is nothing more than an idealistic fantasy, and one that would seek to legitimize the injection of millions of euros into the European military-industrial complex in the form of research and development in order to produce new technology and military and security equipment. This idea may well be implemented in the shape of a European joint force, one that is solely accountable for its missions to an executive body that is unhindered by public pressure that may oppose European participation in irremediably unjust wars and military adventures that will inevitably be anything other than a last resort.

The role of nuclear weapons in the search for a hypothetical military excellence, i.e. one that seeks to attain its idealized stage in the paradigm of deterrence that stems from the mere possession of nuclear weapons themselves should not be ignored. Time has demonstrated the high economic cost that the upkeep, development and dismantling of such a deterrent has entailed. Military budgets in those countries that possess nuclear weapons are the highest in the world, not only in absolute but also in relative terms. As such these budgets must include, if possible, and with greater urgency than that applied to other expenses, an analysis of the economic efficiency with respect to the decision to maintain nuclear weapons – arms that do not provide greater safety to those who possess them, but that rather give rise to greater risks, i.e. those that derive from accidents relating to their very ownership.

In short, the amount of military spending made in any given country gives rise to an equation in which the industrial military complex appears as one of the most heavily weighted variables. The interest of this sector with respect to budgetary increases allocated to the future acquisition of its products and services is more than obvious. Another key variable is that created by transnational companies, among which those dedicated to extractive means of production are the most noteworthy, and it is precisely companies of this type that benefit from most of those military missions embarked on abroad. Many of the budgetary increases provided to this sector may only be explained as a means to counter potential threats to supplies of energy and raw materials with respect to those economies that depend on highly globalized production means. The impact of the combination of both these factors in promoting and maintaining a global economy that is responsible for creating one of the main threats of our time, that of climate change, is again, more than evident.

The decision-making process hidden behind military spending includes the active role of all those actors who benefit from this expenditure – this includes both those private companies that need arms production to survive, and those economic sectors that use military power to maintain and expand their activities, and these actors all play leading roles. To ensure the success of their actions they implement lobbying strategies that focus on those governments and parliamentary bodies that influence decisions on the expenses allocated to military budgets. However, it is not only the private business sector that seeks to exert its weight on matters of military spending, civil society also tries to sway rulers and society in general. Hundreds of pacifist organizations attempt to inform society of the need to reduce military expenditure in order to achieve higher levels of peace and security with regard to armed conflicts, and seek to encourage a more efficient use of public resources in order to respond to those matters that actually do threaten the security of ordinary people; issues that include climate change, poverty or disease, among others.

Since 2009 the pacifist organization, and holder of the Nobel Peace Prize, International Peace Bureau, which is responsible for coordinating the Centre Delàs for Peace Studies in Barcelona, has been coordinating the tasks of the Global Campaign on Military Spending (GCOMS) and has been promoting the task of independent advocacy, and has sought to unite all those public voices opposed to increased military spending. This is an enormous task, one which, in terms of resources to exerting pressure on governments, it stands to lose. Nonetheless, like all the work carried out by social movements, it may bear fruit as soon as it reaches a sufficient level of recognition, or perhaps it has already served as a counterbalance to still higher increases in military spending. As with other areas of social mobilization, an analysis of the efforts applied to reducing those resources allocated to militarization may only be accurately made over a period of years. Environmentalism and Feminism already seem to have become pervasive in many public policies that are now implemented by governments around the world, perhaps the next social movement to do the same will be Pacifism.

Index

Printed in the United States
By Bookmasters